I Am Malala

I Am Malala

How One Girl Stood Up
for Education and
Changed the World

MALALA YOUSAFZAI
with PATRICIA McCORMICK

Young Readers Edition

Little, Brown and Company
New York   Boston

Little, Brown and Company

Hachette Book Group
1290 Avenue of the Americas, New York, NY 10104
Visit us at lb-kids.com

Little, Brown and Company is a division of Hachette Book Group, Inc.
The Little, Brown name and logo are trademarks of Hachette Book Group, Inc.

First Edition: August 2014

Library of Congress Cataloging-in-Publication Data

Yousafzai, Malala, 1997–
    I am Malala : how one girl stood up for education and changed the world / Malala Yousafzai with Patricia McCormick.—Young readers edition.
        pages cm
    ISBN 978-0-316-32793-0 (hardback)—ISBN 978-0-316-32794-7 (ebook)—ISBN 978-0-316-32792-3 (library edition ebook)   1. Yousafzai, Malala, 1997– —Juvenile literature   2. Young women—Education—Pakistan—Biography—Juvenile literature.   3. Children's rights—Pakistan—Juvenile literature.   I. McCormick, Patricia, 1956–   II. Title.
    LC2330.Y68 2014
    370.82095491—dc23
                                                                2014015881

20 19 18 17 16 15 14

LSC-C

Printed in the United States of America

Typography by Sasha Illingworth

To those children all over the world who have no access to education, to those teachers who bravely continue teaching, and to anyone who has fought for their basic human rights and education.

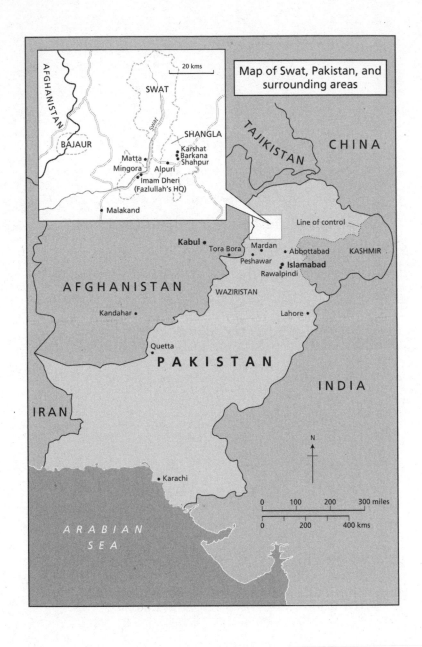

20 kms

SWAT

SHANGLA

AFGHANISTAN

BAJAUR

Karshat
Barkana
Shahpur

Matta
Mingora   Alpuri

Imam Dheri
(Fazlullah's HQ)

Malakand

TAJIKISTAN

CHINA

Map of Swat, Pakistan, and
surrounding areas

Line of control

Kabul   Tora Bora   Mardan

Peshawar   Abbottabad   KASHMIR

Islamabad
Rawalpindi

AFGHANISTAN

WAZIRISTAN

Kandahar   Lahore

Quetta

PAKISTAN

INDIA

IRAN

N

Karachi

0   100   200   300 miles

0   200   400 kms

ARABIAN
SEA

CONTENTS

PROLOGUE

When I close my eyes, I can see my bedroom. The bed is unmade, my fluffy blanket in a heap, because I've rushed out for school, late for an exam. My school schedule is open on my desk to a page dated 9 October 2012. And my school uniform—my white *shalwar* and blue *kamiz*—is on a peg on the wall, waiting for me.

I can hear the neighborhood kids playing cricket in the alley behind our home. I can hear the hum of the bazaar not far away. And if I listen very closely, I can hear Safina, my friend next door, tapping on the wall we share so she can tell me a secret.

I smell rice cooking as my mother works in the kitchen. I hear my little brothers fighting over the remote—the TV switching between *WWE SmackDown* and cartoons. Soon I'll hear my father's deep voice as he calls out my nickname.

"*Jani*," he'll say, which is Persian for "dear one." "How was the school running today?" He was asking how things were at the Khushal School for Girls, which he founded and I attended, but I always took the opportunity to answer the question literally.

"*Aba*," I'd joke. "The school is walking, not running!" This was my way of telling him I thought things could be better.

I left that beloved home in Pakistan one morning—planning to dive back under the covers as soon as school let out—and ended up a world away.

Some people say it is too dangerous for me to go back there now. That I'll never be able to return. And so, from time to time, I go there in my mind.

But now another family lives in that home, another girl sleeps in that bedroom—while I am thousands of miles away. I don't care much about the other things in my room, but I do worry about the school trophies on my bookcase. I even dream about them sometimes. There's a runners-up award from the first speaking contest I ever entered. And more than forty-five golden cups and medals for being first in my class in exams, debates, and competitions. To someone else, they might seem mere trinkets made of plastic. To someone else, they may simply look like prizes for good grades. But to me, they are reminders of the life I loved and the girl I was—before I left home that fateful day.

When I open my eyes, I am in my new bedroom. It is in a sturdy brick house in a damp and chilly place called

Birmingham, England. Here there is water running from every tap, hot or cold as you like. No need to carry cans of gas from the market to heat the water. Here there are large rooms with shiny wood floors, filled with large furniture and a large, large TV.

There is hardly a sound in this calm, leafy suburb. No children laughing and yelling. No women downstairs chopping vegetables and gossiping with my mother. No men smoking cigarettes and debating politics. Sometimes, though, even with these thick walls between us, I can hear someone in my family crying for home. But then my father will burst through the front door, his voice booming. "*Jani!*" he'll say. "How was school today?"

Now there's no play on words. He's not asking about the school he runs and I attend. But there's a note of worry in his voice, as if he fears I won't be there to reply. Because it was not so long ago that I was nearly killed—simply because I was speaking out about my right to go to school.

———

It was the most ordinary of days. I was fifteen, in grade nine, and I'd stayed up far too late the night before, studying for an exam.

I'd already heard the rooster crow at dawn but had fallen back to sleep. I'd heard the morning call to prayer from the mosque nearby but managed to hide under my quilt. And I'd pretended not to hear my father come to wake me.

Then my mother came and gently shook my shoulder. "Wake up, *pisho*," she said, calling me *kitten* in Pashto, the language of the Pashtun people. "It's seven thirty and you're late for school!"

I had an exam on Pakistani studies. So I said a quick prayer to God. *If it is your will, may I please come in first?* I whispered. *Oh, and thank you for all my success so far!*

I gulped down a bit of fried egg and chapati with my tea. My youngest brother, Atal, was in an especially cheeky mood that morning. He was complaining about all the attention I'd received for speaking out about girls getting the same education as boys, and my father teased him a little at the breakfast table.

"When Malala is prime minister someday, you can be her secretary," he said.

Atal, the little clown in the family, pretended to be cross. "No!" he cried. "She will be *my* secretary!"

All this banter nearly made me late, and I raced out the door, my half-eaten breakfast still on the table. I ran down the lane just in time to see the school bus crammed with other girls on their way to school. I jumped in that Tuesday morning and never looked back at my home.

———

The ride to school was quick, just five minutes up the road and along the river. I arrived on time, and exam day passed as it always did. The chaos of Mingora city surrounded us with its honking horns and factory noises while we worked silently, bent over our papers in hushed concentration. By day's end I was tired but happy; I knew I'd done well on my test.

"Let's stay on for the second trip," said Moniba, my best friend. "That way we can chat a little longer." We always liked to stay on for the late pickup.

For days I'd had a strange, gnawing feeling that something bad was going to happen. One night I'd found myself wondering about death. *What is being dead really like?* I wanted to know. I was alone in my room, so I turned toward Mecca and asked God. "What happens when you die?" I said. "How would it feel?"

If I died, I wanted to be able to tell people what it felt like. "Malala, you silly girl," I said to myself then, "you'd be dead and you couldn't tell people what it was like."

Before I went to bed, I asked God for one more thing. *Can I die a little bit and come back, so I can tell people about it?*

But the next day had dawned bright and sunny, and so had the next one and the one after that. And now I knew I'd done well on my exam. Whatever cloud had been hanging over my head had begun to clear away. So Moniba and I did what we always did: We had a good gossip. What face cream was she using? Had one of the male teachers gone for a baldness cure? And, now that the first exam was over, how difficult would the next one be?

When our bus was called, we ran down the steps. As usual,

Moniba and the other girls covered their heads and faces before we stepped outside the gate and got into the waiting *dyna*, the white truck that was our Khushal School "bus." And, as usual, our driver was ready with a magic trick to amuse us. That day, he made a pebble disappear. No matter how hard we tried, we couldn't figure out his secret.

We piled inside, twenty girls and two teachers crammed into the three rows of benches stretching down the length of the *dyna*. It was hot and sticky, and there were no windows, just a yellowed plastic sheet that flapped against the side as we bounced along Mingora's crowded rush-hour streets.

Haji Baba Road was a jumble of brightly colored rick-shaws, women in flowing robes, men on scooters, honking and zigzagging through the traffic. We passed a shopkeeper butch-ering chickens. A boy selling ice-cream cones. A billboard for Dr. Humayun's Hair Transplant Institute. Moniba and I were deep in conversation. I had many friends, but she was the friend of my heart, the one with whom I shared everything. That day, when we were talking about who would get the high-est marks this term, one of the other girls started a song, and the rest of us joined in.

Just after we passed the Little Giants snack factory and the bend in the road not more than three minutes from my house, the van slowed to a halt. It was oddly quiet outside.

"It's so calm today," I said to Moniba. "Where are all the people?"

I don't remember anything after that, but here's the story that's been told to me:

Two young men in white robes stepped in front of our truck.

"Is this the Khushal School bus?" one of them asked.

The driver laughed. The name of the school was painted in black letters on the side.

The other young man jumped onto the tailboard and leaned into the back, where we were all sitting.

"Who is Malala?" he asked.

No one said a word, but a few girls looked in my direction. He raised his arm and pointed at me. Some of the girls screamed, and I squeezed Moniba's hand.

Who is Malala? I am Malala, and this is my story.

PART ONE

Before the Taliban

1

As Free as a Bird

I am Malala, a girl like any other—although I do have my special talents.

I am double-jointed, and I can crack the knuckles on my fingers and my toes at will. (And I enjoy watching people squirm as I do it.) I can beat someone twice my age at arm wrestling. I like cupcakes but not candy. And I don't think dark chocolate should be called chocolate at all. I hate eggplant and green peppers, but I love pizza. I think Bella from *Twilight* is too fickle, and I don't understand why she would choose that boring Edward. As my girlfriends in Pakistan and I say, he doesn't give her any lift.

Now, I don't care much for makeup and jewelry, and I'm not a girly girl. But my favorite color is pink, and I do admit I used to spend a lot of time in front of the mirror playing with my hair. And when I was younger, I tried to lighten my skin with honey, rose water, and buffalo milk. (When you put milk on your face, it smells very bad.)

I say that if you check a boy's backpack, it will always be a mess, and if you check his uniform, it will be dirty. This is not my opinion. This is just a fact.

I am a Pashtun, a member of a proud tribe of people spread across Afghanistan and Pakistan. My father, Ziauddin, and my mother, Toor Pekai, are from mountain villages, but after they married, they relocated to Mingora, the largest city in the Swat Valley, which is in northwest Pakistan, where I was born. Swat was known for its beauty, and tourists came from all over to see its tall mountains, lush green hills, and crystal-clear rivers.

I'm named for the great young Pashtun heroine Malalai, who inspired her countrymen with her courage.

But I don't believe in fighting—even though my fourteen-year-old brother, Khushal, annoys me to no end. *I* don't fight with him. Rather, *he* fights with me. And I agree with Newton: For every action, there is an equal and opposite reaction. So I guess you could say that when Khushal fights with me, I oblige him. We argue over the TV remote. Over chores. Over who's the better student. Over who ate the last of the Cheesy Wotsits. Over whatever you can think of.

My ten-year-old brother, Atal, annoys me less. And he is quite good at chasing down the cricket ball when we kick it out of bounds. But he does make up his own rules sometimes.

When I was younger and these brothers started coming along, I had a little talk with God. *God*, I said, *you did not check with me before sending these two. You didn't ask how I felt. They are quite inconvenient sometimes,* I told God. When I want to study, they make a terrible racket. And when I brush my teeth in the morning, they bang on the bathroom door. But I have made my peace with these brothers. At least with a pair of them, we can play a cricket match.

At home in Pakistan, the three of us ran like a pack of rabbits, in and out of the alleys around our house; we played a chasing game like tag, another game called Mango, Mango, a hopscotch game we called *Chindakh* (meaning "Frog"), and Thief and Police. Sometimes we rang the bell at someone else's house, then ran away and hid. Our favorite, though, was cricket. We played cricket day and night in the alley by our house or up on our roof, which was flat. If we couldn't afford a proper cricket ball, we made one out of an old sock stuffed with rubbish; and we drew wickets on the wall in chalk. Because Atal was the youngest, he would be sent to fetch the ball when it sailed off the roof; sometimes he grabbed the neighbors' ball while he was at it. He'd return with a cheeky grin and a shrug. "What's wrong?" he'd say. "They took our ball yesterday!"

But boys are, well, boys. Most of them are not as civilized as girls. And so, if I wasn't in the mood for their boyish ways, I'd go downstairs and knock on the wall between our house and Safina's. Two taps, that was our code. She'd tap in reply. I'd slip aside a brick, opening a hole between our houses, and we'd whisper back and forth. Sometimes we'd go over to one house or the other, where we'd watch our favorite TV show, *Shaka Laka Boom Boom*—about a boy with a magic pencil. Or we'd work on the little shoebox dolls we were making out of matchsticks and bits of fabric.

Safina was my playmate from the time I was about eight. She's a couple of years younger than me, but we were very close. We sometimes copied each other, but one time I thought she had gone too far, when my favorite possession—my only toy, a pink plastic cell phone my father had given me—went missing.

That afternoon, when I went to play with Safina, she had an identical phone! She said it was hers; she said she'd bought it at the bazaar. Well, I didn't believe her, and I was too angry to think straight. So when she wasn't looking, I took a pair of her earrings. The next day, a necklace. I didn't even like these trinkets, but I couldn't stop myself.

A few days later I came home to find my mother so upset she wouldn't look at me. She had found the stolen trinkets in my small cupboard and had returned them. "Safina stole from me first!" I cried. But my mother was unmoved. "You are older, Malala. You should have set a good example." I went to my room, drenched in shame. But it was the long wait for my father to come home that was worse. He was my hero—brave and principled—and I was his *jani*. He would be so disappointed in me.

But he didn't raise his voice or scold me. He knew I was being so hard on myself already that he had no need to reprimand me. Instead, he consoled me by telling me about the mistakes great heroes had made when they were children. Heroes like Mahatma Gandhi, the great pacifist, and Mohammad Ali Jinnah, the founder of Pakistan. He relayed a saying from a story his father used to tell him: "A child is a child when he's a child, even if he's a prophet."

I thought of our *Pashtunwali* code, which governs how we Pashtuns live. One part of that code is *badal*—a tradition of revenge—where one insult must be answered by another, one death by another, and on and on it goes.

I had had my taste of exacting revenge. And it was bitter. I vowed then that I would never partake in *badal*.

I apologized to Safina and her parents. I hoped Safina would apologize, too, and return my phone. But she didn't say a thing. And, as difficult as it was to keep my new vow, I didn't mention my suspicion concerning the whereabouts of my phone.

Safina and I quickly got back to being friends, and we and all the neighborhood children were back at our running and chasing games. At that time, we lived in a part of town far from the city center. Behind our house was a grassy lot scattered with mysterious ruins—statues of lions, broken columns of an old *stupa,* and hundreds of enormous stones that looked like giant umbrellas—where, in the summer, we played *parpartuni,* a game of hide-and-seek. In the winter, we made snowmen until our mothers called us in for a cup of hot milky tea and cardamom.

For as long as I can remember, our house had been full of people: neighbors, relatives, and friends of my father's—and a never-ending stream of cousins, male and female. They came from the mountains where my parents grew up or they came from the next town over. Even when we moved from our tiny first house and I got my "own" bedroom, it was rarely my own. There always seemed to be a cousin sleeping on the floor. That's because one of the most important parts of the *Pashtunwali* code is hospitality. As a Pashtun, you always open your door to a visitor.

My mother and the women would gather on our veranda at the back of the house and cook and laugh and talk about new clothes, jewelry, and other ladies in the neighborhood, while my father and the men would sit in the men's guest room and drink tea and talk politics.

I would often wander away from the children's games, tip-toe through the women's quarters, and join the men. That, it seemed to me, was where something exciting and important was happening. I didn't know what it was, exactly, and I certainly didn't understand the politics, but I felt a pull to the weighty world of the men. I would sit at my father's feet and drink in the conversation. I loved to hear the men debate politics. But mostly I loved sitting among them, hypnotized by this talk of the big world beyond our valley.

Eventually I'd leave the room and linger awhile among

the women. The sights and sounds in their world were different. There were gentle, confiding whispers. Tinkling laughter sometimes. Raucous, uproarious laughter sometimes. But most stunning of all: The women's headscarves and veils were gone. Their long dark hair and pretty faces—made up with lipstick and henna—were lovely to see.

I had seen these women nearly every day of my life observing the code of *purdah*, where they cover themselves in public. Some, like my mother, simply draped scarves over their faces; this is called *niqab*. But others wore *burqas*, long, flowing black robes that covered the head and face, so people could not even see their eyes. Some went so far as to wear black gloves and socks so that not a bit of skin was showing. I'd seen the wives be required to walk a few paces behind their husbands. I'd seen the women be forced to lower their gaze when they encountered a man. And I'd seen the older girls who'd been our playmates disappear behind veils as soon as they became teenagers.

But to see these women chatting casually—their faces radiant with freedom—was to see a whole new world.

I was never much of a hand around the kitchen—I'll admit that I tried to get out of chopping vegetables or cleaning dishes whenever I could—so I didn't linger there long. But as I ran off, I'd always wonder how it felt to live in hiding.

Living under wraps seemed so unfair—and uncomfortable. From an early age, I told my parents that no matter what other girls did, *I* would never cover my face like that. My face was my identity. My mother, who is quite devout and traditional, was shocked. Our relatives thought I was very bold. (Some said rude.) But my father said I could do as I wished. "Malala will live as free as a bird," he told everyone.

So I would run to rejoin the children. Especially when it was time for the kite-flying contests—where the boys would skillfully try to cut their competitors' kite strings. It was an exciting game, full of unpredictable escapes and plunges. It was beautiful, and also a bit melancholy for me to see the pretty kites sputter to the ground.

Maybe it was because I could see a future that would be cut down just like those kites—simply because I was a girl. Despite what my father said, I knew that as Safina and I got older, we'd be expected to cook and clean for our brothers. We could become doctors because female doctors were needed to care for female patients. But we couldn't be lawyers or engineers, fashion designers or artists—or anything else we dreamed of. And we wouldn't be allowed to go outside our homes without a male relative to accompany us.

As I watched my brothers run up to the roof to launch their kites, I wondered how free I could ever really be.

But I knew, even then, that I was the apple of my father's eye. A rare thing for a Pakistani girl.

When a boy is born in Pakistan, it's cause for celebration. Guns are fired in the air. Gifts are placed in the baby's cot. And the boy's name is inscribed on the family tree. But when a girl is born, no one visits the parents, and women have only sympathy for the mother.

My father paid no mind to these customs. I've seen my name—in bright blue ink—right there among the male names of our family tree. Mine was the first female name in three hundred years.

Throughout my childhood, he sang me a song about my famous Pashtun namesake. "*O Malalai of Maiwand*," he'd sing. "*Rise once more to make Pashtuns understand the song of honor. Your poetic words turn worlds around. I beg you, rise again.*" When I was young, I didn't understand what any of this meant. But as I grew up, I understood that Malalai was a hero and a role model, and I wanted to learn something from her.

And when I started learning to read at age five, my father would brag to his friends. "Look at this girl," he'd say. "She is destined for the skies!" I pretended to be embarrassed, but my father's words of praise have always been the most precious thing in the world to me.

I was far luckier than most girls in one other way, too: My father ran a school. It was a humble place with nothing more than blackboards and chalk—and it was right next to a smelly river. But to me it was a paradise.

My parents tell me that even before I could talk, I would toddle into the empty classrooms and lecture. I delivered lessons in my own baby talk. Sometimes I'd get to sit in on classes with the older children, in awe as I listened to everything they were being taught. As I grew, I longed to wear the uniforms I saw the big girls wearing when they arrived each day: *shalwar kamiz*—a long deep blue tunic and loose white pants—and white headscarf.

My father started the school three years before I was born, and he was teacher, accountant, and principal—as well as janitor, handyman, and chief mechanic. He climbed up the ladder to change the lightbulbs and down the well when the pump broke. When I saw him disappear down that well, I wept, thinking he would never come back. Although I didn't understand it at the time, I know now that there was never enough money. After paying the rent and salaries, there was not much left for food, so we often had little for dinner. But the school had been my father's dream, and we were all happy to be living it.

When it was finally time for me to go to classes, I was so excited I could hardly contain myself. You could say I grew up in a school. The school was my world, and my world was the school.

2

Dreams

Every spring and fall, during the holidays of Big Eid and Small Eid, my family visited one of my favorite places on earth: Shangla, the mountain village where my parents grew up. Laden with presents for our relatives—embroidered shawls, boxes of rose and pistachio sweets, and medicines they couldn't get in the village—we'd go to the Mingora bus station and see just about everybody else in town all crowded together and waiting for the Flying Coach.

We'd stack our gifts—along with the sacks of flour and sugar, blankets, and trunks that other families were taking— on top of the bus in a great towering pile. Then we all crammed inside for the four-hour trip up winding, rutted roads to the mountains. For the first quarter of the journey, the road was a series of zigs and zags that followed the Swat River on one side and hugged sheer cliffs on the other. My brothers took great pleasure in pointing out the wreckage of vehicles that had fallen into the valley below.

The Flying Coach would climb higher and higher, until the air turned cool and crisp. Eventually we saw nothing but mountain after mountain. Mountain, mountain, mountain, and just a sliver of sky.

Many of the people in Shangla were very poor and did not have modern facilities, such as hospitals and markets, but our family always put on a huge feast for us when we arrived. A feast that was especially welcome at Small Eid, which marks the end of a month of daytime fasting for Ramadan. There were bowls of chicken and rice, spinach and lamb, big crunchy apples, pretty yellow cakes, and big kettles of sweet milky tea.

Even when I was only seven or eight, I was considered a sophisticated city girl, and sometimes my cousins teased me because I didn't like to go barefoot and I wore clothes bought at the bazaar, not homemade like theirs. I had a city accent and spoke city slang, so they thought I was modern. If only they knew. People from real cities like Peshawar or Islamabad would have thought *me* very backward.

When I was in the village, though, I lived the life of a country girl. In the morning, I got up when the rooster crowed or when I heard the clatter of dishes as the women downstairs made breakfast for the men. Then all the children spilled out of the houses to greet the day. We ate honey straight from the hive and green plums sprinkled with salt. None of us had any toys or books, so we played hopscotch and cricket in a gully.

In the afternoon the boys would go off fishing while we girls went down to a stream to play our favorite game: Wedding. We would choose a bride and then prepare her for the ceremony. We draped her in bangles and necklaces and painted her face with makeup and her hands with henna. Once she was ready to be given to the groom, she would pretend to cry, and we would stroke her hair and tell her not to worry. Sometimes we would fall down laughing.

But life for the women in the mountains was not easy. There were no proper shops, no universities, no hospitals or female doctors, no clean water or electricity from the government. Many of the men had left the villages to work on road crews and in mines far, far away, sending money home when they could. Sometimes the men never made it back.

The women of the village also had to hide their faces whenever they left their homes. And they could not meet or speak to men who were not their close relatives. None of them could read. Even my own mother, who'd grown up in the village, couldn't read. It is not at all uncommon for women in my country to be illiterate, but to see my mother, a proud and intelligent woman, struggle to read the prices in the bazaar was an unspoken sadness for both of us, I think.

Many of the girls in the village—including most of my own cousins—didn't go to school. Some fathers don't even think of their daughters as valued members of their families, because they'll be married off at a young age to live with their husband's family. "Why send a daughter to school?" the men often say. "She doesn't need an education to run a house."

I would never talk back to my elders. In my culture, one must never disrespect one's elders—even if they are wrong.

But when I saw how hard these women's lives were, I was confused and sad. Why were women treated so poorly in our country?

I asked my father this, and he told me that life was even worse for women in Afghanistan, where a group called the Taliban had taken over the country. Schools for girls had been burned to the ground, and all women were forced to wear a severe form of *burqa*, a head-to-toe veil that had only a tiny fabric grille for their eyes. Women were banned from laughing out loud or wearing nail polish, and they were beaten or jailed for walking without a male family member.

I shuddered when he told me such things and thanked God that I lived in Pakistan, where a girl was free to go to school.

It was the first time I'd heard of the Taliban. What I didn't realize was that they weren't only in Afghanistan. There was another group in Pakistan, not far away in the tribal belt (known as the FATA). Some of them were Pashtuns, like us, and they would soon come to cast a dark shadow over my sunny childhood.

But my father told me not to worry. "I will protect your freedom, Malala," he said. "Carry on with your dreams."

3

A Magic Pencil

By the time I was eight years old, my father had more than eight hundred students and three campuses—an elementary division and two high schools, one for boys and one for girls—so our family finally had enough money to buy a TV. That's when I became obsessed with owning a magic pencil. I got the idea from *Shaka Laka Boom Boom*, the show Safina and I watched after school. It was about a boy named Sanju, who could make anything real by drawing it. If he was hungry, he drew a bowl of curry, and it appeared. If he was in danger, he drew a policeman. He was a little hero, always protecting people who were in danger.

At night I would pray, *God, please give me Sanju's pencil. I won't tell anyone. Just leave it in my cupboard. I will use it to make everyone happy.* As soon as I finished praying, I would check the drawer. But the pencil was never there.

One afternoon the boys weren't home and my mother asked me to throw away some potato peels and eggshells. I walked to the dump, just a block or so from our house, wrinkling my nose as I got close, swatting away flies, and making sure I didn't step on anything in my nice shoes. If only I had Sanju's magic pencil. I would erase it all: the smell, the rats, the giant mountain of rotting food. As I tossed our rubbish onto the heap, I saw something move. I jumped.

It was a girl my age. Her hair was matted and her skin was covered in sores. She was sorting rubbish into piles, one for cans, one for bottles. Nearby, boys were fishing in the pile for metal using magnets on strings. I wanted to talk to them, but I was scared.

Later that day, when my father returned home, I told him about the children at the dump and dragged him to see them. He spoke gently to the children, but they ran away. I asked him why they weren't in school. He told me that these children were supporting their families, selling whatever they found for a few rupees; if they went to school, their families would go hungry. As we walked back home, I saw tears on his cheek.

I believe there is something good for every evil, that every time there's a bad person, God sends a good one. So I decided it was time to talk to God about this problem. *Dear God,* I wrote in a letter. *Did you know there are children who are forced to work in the rubbish heap?* I stopped. Of course he knew! Then I realized that it was his will that *I* had seen them. He was showing me what my life might be like if I couldn't go to school.

Until then, I had believed a magic pencil could change the world. Now I knew *I* would have to do something. I didn't know what it was. But I asked God for *the strength and courage to make the world a better place.* I signed my letter, rolled it up, tied it to a piece of wood, placed a dandelion on top, and floated it in a stream that flows into the Swat River. Surely God would find it there.

As much as I wanted to help the children from the dump, my mother wanted to help everyone. She had started putting bread crusts in a bowl on the kitchen windowsill. Nearby was an extra pot of rice and chicken. The bread was for the birds; the food was for a poor family in our neighborhood.

I asked her once why she always gave food away. "We have known what it is like to be hungry, *pisho*," she said. "We must never forget to share what we have."

So we shared *every*thing we had. We even shared our home with a family of seven who had fallen on hard times. They were supposed to pay my father rent, but more often than not, he ended up lending them money. And although my father's school wasn't really making a profit, he gave away more than a hundred free places to poor children. He wished he could have given away more. My mother, meanwhile, started serving a few girls breakfast at our house each day. "How can they learn," she said, "if their stomachs are empty?"

One day I noticed that some of our longtime students had not returned. I asked my father where they were. "Oh, *jani*," he said, "some of the richer parents took their children out of school when they found out they were sharing classrooms with the sons and daughters of people who cleaned their houses or washed their clothes."

I was young, but I was old enough to feel that wasn't right and to understand that if too many paying students left, it would mean hard times for the school and for our family. What I didn't know was that a bigger threat was looming— not just for our family and our school, but for all of Pakistan.

4

A Warning from God

One autumn day when I was still in primary school, our desks started to tremble and shake. "Earthquake!" we yelled. We ran outside, some of us falling as we crowded through the narrow door and gathered around our teachers for safety and comfort, like chicks around a mother hen. A few of the girls were crying.

We lived in a region where earthquakes happened often, but this felt different. Even after we returned to class, the buildings continued to shake; the rumbling didn't stop. Miss Ulfat, my all-time favorite teacher, told us to stay calm. She assured us that it would soon be over. But when another strong earthquake hit within a few minutes of the first, the students were sent home.

When I arrived home, I found my mother sitting in the courtyard (where she felt safest because there was no roof above her). She was reciting verses from the Holy Quran as tears streamed down her face. The aftershocks kept coming and continued past nightfall, and every time they did, my mother ran outside and insisted we go with her. My father told her to not upset the children, but we were already upset because the ground was shaking!

That earthquake of 8 October 2005 turned out to be one of the worst in history. It was 7.6 on the Richter scale and was felt as far away as Kabul and Delhi. Aftershocks continued for at least a month. Our city of Mingora was largely spared, but the northern areas of Pakistan, including our beloved Shangla, were devastated.

When we finally heard from our family and friends there, they said they had thought it was the end of the world. They described the roar of rocks sliding down hills and everyone running out of their houses reciting the Holy Quran, the screams as roofs crashed down and the howls of buffalo and goats. They were terrified; and then when the destruction stopped, they waited for help.

The government was slow to arrive, but help came immediately from rescue workers from a conservative religious group called Tehrik-e-Nifaz-e-Sharia-e-Mohammadi (TNSM), or the Movement for the Enforcement of Islamic Law, led by Sufi Mohammad and his son-in-law, Maulana Fazlullah.

Eventually the government tried to help, and aid from the Americans (who had troops and helicopters in nearby Afghanistan) made it in. But most of the volunteers and medical help came from organizations that were linked with militant groups like the TNSM. They helped clear and rebuild destroyed villages. They led prayers and buried bodies. They took in many of the eleven thousand orphaned children. In our culture, orphans are usually adopted by the extended family, but the earthquake had been so bad that entire families had been wiped out or lost everything and were in no position to care for additional children. Many of the orphans went to live in fundamentalist madrasas.

Mullahs from the TNSM preached that the earthquake was a warning from God. If we did not mend our ways and introduce *sharia*, or Islamic law, more severe punishment would come.

The whole country was in shock for a long time after the earthquake. We were vulnerable. Which made it that much easier for someone with bad intentions to use a nation's fear for his gain.

5

The First Direct Threat

Each morning, as my friends passed through the gate to school, a man across the street stood scowling at us. Then one night he arrived at our home, along with six elders from the community. I answered the door. He claimed to be a *mufti*, or an Islamic scholar, and said he had a problem with the school. My father shooed me into the other room as this *mufti* and the elders crowded into our little house, but I heard every word.

"I am representing good Muslims," the *mufti* said. "And we all think your girls' high school is a blasphemy. You should close it. Teenage girls should not be going to school. They should be in *purdah*." This *mufti* was clearly under the influence of a *maulana* who had been running an illegal radio broadcast through which he gave sermons and railed against people whom he deemed "un-Islamic."

What we knew, but the *mufti* did not, was that his own niece attended my father's school in secret.

As my father debated with the *mufti*, one of the elders spoke up. "I'd heard you were not a pious man," the man said to my father. "But there are Qurans here in your home."

"Of course there are!" my father said. "I am a Muslim."

The *mufti* jumped back into the conversation, complaining about girls entering the school through the same gate that men also used. So my father came up with a compromise: The older girls would enter through a different gate.

Eventually the *mufti* backed down and the men left. But even as the door shut behind them, I had a knot in my stomach. I had grown up watching stubborn, prideful Pashtun men. Generally, when a Pashtun man loses an argument, he never really forgets. Or forgives.

Even though I was a child, I knew this man was mistaken. I had studied the Quran, our holy book, since I was five; and my parents sent me to a madrasa for religious studies in the afternoons when school finished. It was an open-air mosque where boys and girls studied the Holy Quran together. I loved learning the Arabic alphabet. I loved the strange and mysterious shapes of the letters, the sounds of the prayers as we all recited together, and the stories about how to live a life according to the teachings of Allah.

My teacher there was a woman. She was kind and wise. For me, the madrasa was a place for religious education only; I would go to the Khushal School for all my other studies. But for many of these children, the madrasa would be the only place they would ever study. They wouldn't take any other classes: no science, no math, no literature. They would study only Arabic so that they could recite the Holy Quran. They didn't learn what the words actually meant, though, only how to say them.

I didn't think much of this difference until later, after the mufti's visit to our house. One day I was playing with the neighborhood children in the alley, and when we were choosing up sides for a game of cricket, one of the boys said he didn't want me on his team.

"Our school is better than yours," he said, as if that explained things.

I didn't agree one bit. "My school is the better one," I said.

"Your school is bad," he insisted. "It is not on the straight path of Islam."

I didn't know what to make of this, but I knew he was wrong. My school was a heaven.

Because inside the Khushal School, we flew on wings of knowledge. In a country where women aren't allowed out in public without a man, we girls traveled far and wide inside the pages of our books. In a land where many women can't read the prices in the markets, we did multiplication. In a place where, as soon as we were teenagers, we'd have to cover our heads and hide ourselves from the boys who'd been our childhood playmates, we ran as free as the wind.

We didn't know where our education would take us. All

we wanted was a chance to learn in peace. And that is what we did. The crazy world could carry on outside the walls of the Khushal School. Inside, we could be who we were.

Our only concerns, once we dropped our schoolbags in the classroom, were the same as any child's at school: Who would get the highest grade on the day's test, and who would sit with whom at recess?

It was a point of pride for me that almost every year in primary school, I won the trophy for first place at the end of the term. I was considered one of the top girls—and the principal's daughter—and some girls thought maybe there was a connection between the two. But it was a point of pride for my father that he gave me no special treatment. And the proof was obvious to everyone when a new girl came to school when I was about nine.

Her name was Malka-e-Noor, and she was bright and determined, but I did not think she was nearly as clever as me. So on the last day of school that year, when the awards were announced, I was stunned. She had gotten first place and I was second.

I smiled politely as she received her trophy, but the minute I got home I burst into tears. When my father saw me, he comforted me, but not in the way I wanted. "It's a good thing to come in second," he said. "Because you learn that if you can win, you can lose. And you should learn to be a good loser, not just a good winner."

I was too young—and too stubborn—to appreciate his

words. (And, truth be told, I still prefer to be first.) But after that term, I worked extra hard so I would never have to learn that particular lesson again!

Another of my regular worries was whether Moniba was angry with me. She was my best friend, bookish like me, almost like my twin. We sat together whenever we could—on the bus, at recess, in the classroom—and she made me laugh as no one else could. But we had a habit of fighting, and always over the same thing: when another girl came between us.

"Are you my friend or hers?" Moniba would say if I sat with another girl at recess.

"Moniba," I'd say, "you were the one ignoring me!"

The worst part was when Moniba would refuse to talk to me. Then I would get angry at her for being so angry at me! Sometimes these spats would last for days. Eventually I would miss her too much and I would take responsibility for the fight. (I seemed to always take the blame!) Then she would make a funny face, and we'd fall apart laughing and forget our differences. Until the next time another girl came between us.

How could a place where I learned so much and laughed so much be bad?

PART TWO

A Shadow over Our Valley

6

Radio Mullah

I was at the home of one of my relatives in Mingora one evening when I heard a strange sobbing coming from the radio.

After a long day of cooking, the women had gathered around the radio as they cleaned up. As usual, I was doing my best to get out of having to do the dishes, but I stopped at the sound of this odd weeping.

At first, it sounded like just another *imam* giving advice about how to live a virtuous life. Quit smoking, he told the men. And pray daily. The women murmured in approval, my mother among them.

Then he began to cry. *Stop listening to music*, he begged. *Stop going to movies. Stop dancing. Stop*, he begged, *or God will send another earthquake to punish us all.* Some of the women began to cry. Terrifying memories of the earthquake the previous year were fresh in their minds; some of them had buried children and husbands and were still grieving.

I knew what this radio *mullah* was saying wasn't true. An earthquake is a geological event that can be explained by science, I wanted to tell them. But these women, many of whom had no education and who were brought up to follow the dictates of their religious leaders, were frightened. As the *mullah* wept, so did they.

Even at school, all that my friends could talk about was the Radio Mullah, although my father told us not to listen. Our old radio was broken, so I hadn't heard his latest broadcasts, but I heard them at friends' and relatives' houses, and my friends at school repeated his nightly sermons almost word for word. All music was *haram*, he said, forbidden by Islam. Only his radio station was permitted. Men should grow their hair and beards long, not keep them short, in what he called the "innovative" fashion. And women, he said, should stay at home in *purdah* quarters at all times: They should go out only in emergencies and only wearing a *burqa* and only with a male relative.

At first, my mother had enjoyed his sermons when she listened to them with our relatives—especially when he spoke about the need for daily prayer. People, especially women, romanticized him. People thought he was a good interpreter of the Holy Quran and admired his charisma. They liked his talk of bringing back Islamic law, because everyone was frustrated with the slow, corrupt Pakistani justice system. His followers chanted poems that sounded beautiful but were in fact messages to motivate girls to stop going to school.

My father disapproved of him from the beginning.

"No Radio Mullah is going to tell me what to do. "This '*mullah*,'" he declared, "is nonsense and trouble."

"Don't speak that way," my mother told him. "God will be angry with you."

My father turned out to be right.

He had done some investigating of the man behind the mysterious radio voice. "This '*mullah*' is a high school drop-out! He doesn't even have religious credentials! This so-called *mullah* is spreading ignorance."

The voice on the radio belonged to Maulana Fazlullah, one of the leaders of the TNSM. His followers had helped so many people after the earthquake, but he was taking advantage of the trauma to instill fear in them, too.

Soon Fazlullah's attacks became personal. He announced the names of men who'd spoken out against him. People we knew. People we didn't know. People who were campaigning for peace in the valley, but also people who thought they were having private conversations. They were all suddenly— publicly—called sinful. It was as if the Radio Mullah and his men could see through walls.

———————

Now that I was getting older, it wasn't so easy to sit in on the men's discussions without being noticed. So I would offer to serve them tea—if only so I could hear what matters they were discussing.

In those days there were only two topics of conversation: the Radio Mullah and the fighting just across the border in Afghanistan. I was four years old when the 9/11 attacks took place, but I'd grown up hearing the name Osama bin Laden. In our country, everyone knows about 9/11 and Osama bin Laden. It was said that he'd planned those attacks not far away, in Afghanistan, and for the past several years, the United States and its allies had been fighting a war to find him—and to defeat al-Qaeda and the Taliban government in Afghanistan, which was protecting him.

The Taliban. As soon as I would hear that word, my ears would perk up. I'd think back to the conversation I'd had with my father when we were in Shangla. The Taliban seemed like something far away then, something bad in a distant place. Many of my father's friends believed that despite how popular Fazlullah was becoming and his association with the Taliban in Pakistan, they were still too far away to be a concern, but he warned them that there would come a day when the Taliban would reach our valley. "They are already in the tribal belt," he said, "and they are coming nearer." Then he quoted a proverb: "Coming events cast their shadows before."

Fazlullah moved slowly at first, but in the two years that followed the earthquake, he cast a long shadow, indeed. I was growing up, and for the first time it occurred to me that our world was changing before my eyes, and not for the better.

When I went to bed each night, I had a talk with God. *Please, God, tell me what I can do. I'm a small girl, but maybe you have a small job for me?*

I woke up one day with a plan. I would ignore all this Fazlullah gossip when I got to school. My friends and I should be talking about Bella and Edward or Fruity from the Indian TV show *Son Pari*; if those topics were off-limits for the time being, we could talk about cricket or annoying little brothers or a hundred other things.

But when I arrived at school, my friends were all huddled in the corner talking about the latest sermon. The night before, Fazlullah had announced that schools for girls were *haram*. This man had just declared our peaceful sanctuary forbidden by the Holy Quran.

He was only a voice on the radio then. What we didn't know was that he would go much further in his campaign against girls' schools in the days ahead.

7

The Taliban in Swat

The Radio Mullah continued his campaign against anything he deemed un-Islamic and Western. People listened to his broadcasts regularly—many to hear him announce names and make sure theirs weren't on the list. Through his illegal radio broadcasts, he encouraged parents to refuse polio vaccinations for their children. He claimed that this medical aid was not meant to help; he said it was a ploy by Western countries to harm Muslim children.

But he wasn't just interfering with health care and speaking out against girls' schools—he was also threatening barbers who offered so-called Western haircuts and destroying music stores. He persuaded people to donate their jewelry and money, and he used the funds to make bombs and train militants.

We had seen Fazlullah's followers, with their long hair and beards, dressed in black turbans and white *shalwar kamiz*, in the small towns on the way to visit our family in the mountains. His men carried guns and walked menacingly through the streets. But even though we had not seen his men in Mingora proper, we felt his presence. It was as if he spoke from the heavens, casting a dark cloud of fear over our valley.

The police tried to stop him, but his movement was only getting stronger. In May 2007, he signed a peace agreement with the government, saying that he would stop his campaign against polio vaccinations and girls' education, as well as his attacks against government property, and the government would allow him to continue his broadcasts.

In July, everything changed.

Around the time of my tenth birthday, the Pakistani Army led a siege of a women's madrasa in Islamabad, our nation's capital. A group of militants that had been taking an active stance against the government had now taken hostages and hidden inside the madrasa of *Lal Masjid*, or the Red Mosque. After the army's attack, which lasted for days and ended in many deaths, Fazlullah made one of his strangest announcements: He declared war on the government and called for people to rise up in violence. The peace treaty he had signed became nothing more than a memory.

But the government ignored him, like an annoying fly. And it ignored us, too, the people in Swat who were under his thumb. We were angry with our government and angry with these terrorists for trying to ruin our way of life, but my father said our family should do its best to ignore them as well.

"We must live a full life, if only in our hearts," he said. And so, as usual, our family dinner conversations were about things of the mind: Einstein and Newton, the poets and the philosophers. And, as usual, my brothers and I fought over the remote, over who got the best grades, over anything and everything. Somehow I could ignore the Taliban, but I could not ignore these two annoying characters. Fighting with your brothers, I told my father, is also part of a full life!

Soon Fazlullah joined forces with Tehrik-i-Taliban-Pakistan (TTP), or the Pakistan Taliban, and announced that women were banned from public places. The males in the family should enforce this order, he said, and "keep tight control over their families or be punished themselves."

Within six months the streets became strangely absent of women because they were afraid to go out to do their shopping. The DVD shops that sold Bollywood films and children's movies pulled down their shutters and went out of business. Fazlullah claimed that watching movies and TV shows was a sin because it meant that women would look upon men, and men would look upon women, who were forbidden to them.

Under the threat of his followers, people were terrified. Some took their TVs, DVDs, and CDs to the public square, where the Radio Mullah's men set them on fire. Stories spread that his men were patrolling the streets in pickup trucks, shouting his orders from megaphones. Then we heard that his followers were listening at people's doors; if they heard a TV, they bashed the door in and then smashed the TV to bits.

After school, my brothers and I cowered in front of our beloved TV—the volume turned down to a whisper. We adored our shows and didn't understand how wrestlers with funny names and a little boy with a magic pencil were so bad. But every time there was a knock on the door, we jumped. When our father came home one night, I asked him, "*Aba*, will we have to burn our TV as well?"

Eventually we moved our TV to a closet. At least if strangers came to the door, they wouldn't see it.

How had this happened? How did an unschooled fanatic turn himself into a kind of radio god? And why was no one prepared to defy him?

———

Through it all, the Khushal School carried on as usual. A few more of our classmates dropped out, but the rest of us appreciated our schooling all the more. Our class even had a discussion: The government may not be behaving as it should, but could we run our classroom a bit more like a democracy? We hit on an idea: Since the most studious girls always sat up front, we would switch seats every week. If you got to the front row one week, you'd find yourself in the back the next. It was a bit of a game, but it was our small way of saying that all girls—and all people—are equal.

But beyond the walls of our school, Mingora had become like a prison.

Banners that read WOMEN NOT ALLOWED were strung up at the entrance to the market. All music and electronics shops were shut down. Fazlullah even outlawed an old-fashioned children's game called Carrom, where we flicked disks across a wooden board.

He had started announcing the names of schoolgirls on his radio show. "Miss So-and-so has stopped going to school and will go to heaven," he said. Or, "Miss So-and-so has left school, and I congratulate her parents." My mother now insisted that I never walk to school by myself, for fear that I would be seen alone in my school uniform by the Taliban.

Every day, I noticed that a few more of our classmates were missing. And every night on his radio show, Fazlullah kept up his attacks, saying that girls who went to school were not good Muslims—that we would go to hell.

One day one of our teachers went to my father and said he would no longer teach girls. Another said he was leaving to help Fazlullah build a religious center. It was a dark day. The Khushal School, which had always been our refuge, had fallen under the shadow of the Radio Mullah.

Fazlullah had set up a public court to enforce his edicts, and his men were now flogging or killing policemen, government officials, and other men and women who disobeyed him. Hundreds gathered to watch the floggings, shouting *"Allahu akbar"*—God is great!—with each lash. Sometimes, people said, Fazlullah arrived at the proceedings, galloping in on a black horse.

Much of Fazlullah's "justice" was exacted in the dead of

night. Later in his reign of terror, "violators" were dragged from their homes and killed; their bodies would be displayed in the Green Square the next morning. Often a note was pinned to the body: *This is what happens to spies and infidels.*

Or *Do not touch this body until 11 AM or you will be next.* Before long, people had a new name for the Green Square: They started calling it the Bloody Square.

I shuddered to hear these stories. What was becoming of my city? What would become of us?

God, I said when I went to bed, *I know you are busy with many, many things around the world. But do you see what's happening here in Swat?*

One night I overheard my parents talking in hushed voices. "You must do it," my mother said. "To be afraid is no solution."

"I will not go without your blessing," my father said.

"God will protect you," she said. "Because you are speaking the truth."

I stepped out of my hiding place and asked what was going on. My father said he was going to a meeting that night to speak out against the Taliban. And after that he would travel to Islamabad to take the government to task for not protecting its citizens. My father, a simple principal, was taking on the two most powerful and dangerous forces in the country. And my mother was standing by him.

Most Pashtun women would cry and beg and cling to their husbands' sleeves. But most Pashtun men would ignore their wives. Few would have even consulted with them in the first place. But my parents were not like other parents. My father is like a falcon, the one who dared to fly where others would not go. And my mother is the one with her feet firmly planted on the ground.

For my part, I took on the job of locking the house each night when my father was away. I went around the house once, twice, often three times, making sure all the doors and windows were locked. Sometimes my father came home quite late. Sometimes not at all. He took to sleeping at his friends' houses occasionally just in case he was being followed. He was protecting us by staying away, but he could not protect us from worrying. Those nights, I heard my mother praying until all hours.

———————

One day I was traveling to Shangla with my mother and brothers; we didn't own a car, and one of our cousins was giving us a ride. As the traffic slowed to a crawl, he put in a cassette to pass the time. Suddenly he ejected his tape. He scrambled to gather up the other cassettes he kept in the glove box. "Quick," he said to my mother, "hide these in your handbag."

Two men drew near our car. They were wearing black turbans and camouflage vests over their *shalwar kamiz*. They had long hair and beards, and they were carrying Kalashnikov automatic weapons. I was face-to-face with the Taliban.

They were searching cars for anything they claimed was forbidden by Islam. None of us said a word, but I saw my mother's hands shake as she gripped her purse, where the *haram* items were hidden. She pulled her veil more securely across her face and lowered her gaze to her lap.

The Talib leaned in the back window. His eyes bored into mine. "Sisters," he said to both of us, "you must wear a *burqa*. You are bringing shame."

Here was a Talib with a machine gun just inches from my face. How was I bringing shame? I wanted to ask him. I was a child, a ten-year-old girl. A little girl who liked playing hide-and-seek and studying science. I was angry, but I knew it would do no good to try to reason with him. I knew I should have been afraid, but I only felt frustration.

———

When we returned home from that visit to Shangla, we found a letter for my father taped to the school gate.

Sir, the school you are running is Western and infidel, it said. *You teach girls and you have a uniform that is un-Islamic. Stop this or you will be in trouble and your children will weep and cry for you.*

It was signed *Fedayeen of Islam*—devotees of Islam.

The Taliban had threatened my father. Now I was afraid.

8

No One Is Safe

My father replied to the Taliban the next day in a letter to the newspaper.

Please don't harm my schoolchildren, he wrote, *because the God you believe in is the same God they pray to every day. You can take my life, but please don't kill my schoolchildren.*

His letter appeared in the paper—along with his full name and the address of our school—even though my father had written only his name.

Our phone started ringing that night. Friends called to thank my father for speaking up. "You have put the first stone in standing water," one said. "Now many will have the courage to speak up."

But not many people did.

My father had always been a busy man. Participating in *mushaira,* poetry concerts; working late at school; helping neighbors settle disputes. But now when he left home, I felt like that little three-year-old I once was, when he would climb down the ladder at school to fix the well. I wondered each night if he would come back.

After the letter arrived, my father made a decision: The boys at the Khushal School would no longer wear the uniform of shirt and trousers. These supposedly "Western" clothes marked them as identifying with infidels in the eyes of Fazlullah's followers, so, for their safety, he had the boys switch to the traditional tunic and pants of the *shalwar kamiz*. I still wore my blue-and-white *shalwar kamiz*, but the Taliban said girls should not wear the white *shalwar*. The uniform I once loved now made me feel like a criminal. Suddenly, everywhere I looked, the Taliban seemed to sprout like weeds.

Then I thought: *What have I done wrong that I should be afraid? All I want to do is go to school. And that is not a crime. That is my right.* Besides, I was the daughter of Ziauddin Yousafzai, the man who had dared to talk back to the Taliban. I would hold my head high—even if my heart was quaking.

That fall, in October 2007, something happened that gave us hope: Benazir Bhutto, who had been the first female prime minister of Pakistan, was returning to run in that year's election. She had been living in exile in the United Kingdom since I was two years old, but I had been hearing about her for years.

As a woman, she was a role model for girls like me. And she was the only politician who'd had the courage to speak out against the terrorists. Our whole family was glued to the TV when her arrival was broadcast. We watched her weep as she stepped onto Pakistani soil for the first time in almost nine years. My mother was moved by this but was also afraid for her. She said to the TV, "Did you come for death?" Everyone knew it was dangerous for her to return, but we hoped for her safety.

Not long after that, just over two months later, she was dead. It happened right in front of my eyes as I again watched her on TV.

"We will defeat the forces of extremism and militancy with the power of the people," she declared. Then she stood on the seat of her bulletproof vehicle to wave to her supporters.

There was a crack of gunfire and the roar of an explosion. I watched, breathless, as she sank down inside the car. My mother, my father, and my grandmother burst into tears. Benazir Bhutto was the first woman attacked by the terrorists. Despite the fear we all felt for her, we were not expecting them to attack a woman. The killing of women is prohibited by the *Pashtunwali* code. We were shocked.

I found myself oddly still. My first thought was this: *If Benazir Bhutto can die, no one is safe.*

No one *was* safe in Pakistan. Not the women who were forbidden to walk the streets of their own towns. Not the men who were being flogged to death for petty reasons. Not the

As a baby.

As a young child,
being fashionable.

With my brother Khushal in Mingora.

Reading with Khushal.

My paternal grandfather with me
and Khushal in our house in Mingora.

With Khushal, enjoying
the waterfall in Shangla.

Snowfall in Mingora.

A birthday party for my brother Atal
at our house in Mingora.

Playing badminton with my brothers.

The beautiful Swat Valley.

One of the *stupas* of Swat. A *stupa* is a structure believed
to hold ancient relics associated with Buddha.

At the beginning, people gave lots of
money to Maulana Fazlullah.

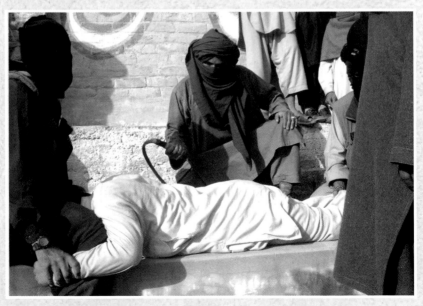

The Taliban publicly whipped people.

Top students getting awards.

Performing in a play at school.

With my school trophies.

A picture I painted when I was twelve, just after we came
back to Swat from being IDPs (internally displaced persons).
It shows the dream of interfaith harmony.

I was voted the class proctor almost every year.

Students outside during a science fair at the Khushal School.

children who worked in the trash heap. Not even children like me who just wanted to go to school.

As I looked at the TV, a tiny voice in my heart whispered to me: "Why don't *you* go there and fight for women's rights? Fight to make Pakistan a better place?"

I had recently done interviews with the TV news channels Dawn and Khyber News about girls' education, and although I had been nervous, I had made it through. And I had liked it.

As everyone around me cried, I kept my secret. I told myself, "I will continue this journey of fighting for peace and democracy in my country."

I was only ten, but I knew then that somehow I would find a way.

9

Candy from the Sky

One day in the autumn of 2007, we were sitting in class when we heard a fearsome roaring from outside. Everyone—students and teachers—ran out to the courtyard and looked up. A swarm of giant black army helicopters darkened the sky overhead. They whipped the wind around us and stirred up a storm of dirt and sand. We cupped our hands over our ears and tried to yell at one another, but our voices were drowned in the din.

Then there was a plunk as something landed on the ground at our feet. *Plunk! Plunk! Plunk!* We screamed—and then we cheered. Toffees! The soldiers were tossing candy down to us. We laughed our heads off as we went scrambling to catch toffees.

We were so delighted that it took us a minute to understand what was going on. The army had come to rescue Swat from Fazlullah! We cheered and clapped and jumped up and down. Candy was falling from the sky! And peace would be coming to Swat!

Soon soldiers were everywhere. Helicopters were even parked on the Mingora golf course. It was strange to see the army in Swat. We'd been praying for someone to stand up to Fazlullah and his men with their black turbans and Kalashnikov rifles. But now our town was swarming with men in green uniforms and Kalashnikov rifles.

Practically overnight Fazlullah's men disappeared, like snow melting into the ground. But although we could not see them anymore, we knew they had not gone far, only a few kilometers away, and Mingora remained a tense and frightened city. Each day after school my brothers and I would race home and lock the doors. No more playing cricket in the alley. No more hide-and-seek in the street. No more candy from the sky.

One evening we heard an announcement from the loudspeakers atop the mosque. The army had imposed a curfew. We didn't know this word, *curfew*, so I knocked on the wall to Safina's house so someone next door would come to the hole in the wall and explain. Soon Safina and her mother and brother came to our house and told us it meant we had to stay indoors for certain hours of the day and always at night. My brothers and I were so scared we didn't even come out of our rooms.

We stayed inside and peered through the curtains at the empty street in front of our house.

That night a streak of bright white light flashed across the sky, lighting the room for a second, like a flashbulb on a camera. *Boom!* A thud shook the ground. I jumped out of bed and ran to my parents. Khushal and Atal came running to join us. We all huddled together, shaking. The dishes clattered, the furniture shook, and the windows rattled. Then, within minutes, the army's gunfire began in the outskirts of the city. With each blast and shot, we gripped one another harder until we drifted off to sleep.

The next morning, we woke up as if we were coming out of a long, fitful dream. After a night full of bombing, the air seemed oddly still. We dared to hope. Was it possible that the army had defeated the Taliban? We peeked out the gate and saw knots of people from the neighborhood gossiping. My father went to find out what had happened. He came back inside, frowning. The rumor on the street: The Taliban were going to take control of Swat. The military operation was ineffective. Our hearts sank.

The army sent ten thousand more men, and the fighting raged on and on, night after night for a year and a half. I was always the first to run to our parents, and my brothers quickly followed. And since the bed was now too crowded, I had to sleep on a pile of blankets on the floor. (Even in the middle of a war, I was able to be irritated with those two for stealing my spot!) Strange as it sounds, we got used to the bombing and shelling. Sometimes Atal slept through it. And Khushal and I came up with a system to figure out where the fighting was. If the fighting was nearby, the electricity went out. If it was farther away, the power stayed on.

There were three types of attacks, and we learned to distinguish them. Bombing was done only by the Taliban, sometimes by remote control, but other times by suicide bombers. Shelling from helicopters and cannons fired from mountaintops was the army. The third type, machine guns, was used by both.

I used to get afraid at night, especially during bomb blasts. From my spot on the floor in my parents' room, I recited a special verse from the Holy Quran, the *Ayat al-Kursi*. Say it three times and your home will be safe from devils and any kind of danger. Say it five times and your neighborhood is safe. Say it seven times and your whole town is safe. I said it seven, eight, nine times, so many times I lost track. Then I spoke to God. *Bless us and protect us*, I'd say. *Bless our father and family.* Then I'd correct myself. *No, bless our street. No, our neighborhood. Bless all of Swat.* Then I'd say, *No, bless all of Pakistan. No, not just Pakistan. Bless all the world.*

I tried to plug my ears and picture my prayers floating up to God. Somehow, each morning, we awoke safe and sound. I didn't know the fate of all the other people I'd prayed for, but I wished for peace for everyone. And, especially, peace for Swat.

One day my prayer was answered. The army hadn't won, but it had at least driven the Taliban into hiding, if not away.

10

2008: What Terrorism Feels Like

Somehow daily life continued despite the bomb blasts and killings. School remained a haven from the insanity of a city in the middle of a war. It wasn't always possible to attend, between the bomb blasts and the curfew (which could be enforced any time of day). And sometimes noisy helicopters flying overhead made it so we couldn't hear a thing, and on those days, we would be sent home. But if the school opened its doors, I was there, ready to spend time with my friends and learn from the teachers.

My friends and I had now moved to the upper school, and our friendly competition got even more competitive. We didn't just want to get good grades; we wanted to get top grades.

It wasn't just that we wanted to be the best—although we each enjoyed it when we were. It was because when our teachers, like Miss Ulfat in primary school, said "Excellent!" or "Well done!" our hearts would fly. Because when a teacher appreciates you, you think, *I am something!* In a society where people believe girls are weak and not capable of anything except cooking and cleaning, you think, *I have a talent.* When a teacher tells you that all great leaders and scientists were once children, too, you think, *Maybe we can be the great ones tomorrow.* In a country where so many people consider it a waste to send girls to school, it is a teacher who helps you believe in your dreams.

And I had found a great new teacher in our upper-school headmistress Madam Maryam. She was bright and independent—everything I wanted to be. She had been to college. She had a job earning her own wage.

Now that we were in upper school, the subjects became more difficult. We took algebra, chemistry, and, my favorite, physics. And even though our teachers had only a blackboard and chalk, we were free to go as far as our curiosity would take us. When we were learning about chemistry, one girl stopped the class to ask a question. "If everything is made up of atoms, what are atoms made of?" Another asked, "If electrons are constantly moving, why isn't this chair I'm sitting on moving?" The teacher put aside the day's lesson plan, and we all asked questions to our hearts' content.

But mostly what we talked about those days was the army and the Taliban. All the people of Swat were caught in the middle. One friend used to like to annoy me by saying, "Taliban is good, army not good." And I would always reply, "When you are caught between military and militants, there is no good."

———————

The trips from school had become tense and frightening, and I just wanted to relax once I was safe inside my home. One day I arrived ahead of my brothers—thrilled I didn't have to fight with Khushal for the remote for once—and settled in to watch my new favorite show, *Shararat*, which means "making mischief." It was just a Bollywood comedy, but I loved it.

I turned on the TV—and all I got was static. I switched stations. More static. I tried every station. Nothing but static. At first, I thought it was another annoying power outage; we'd been having them every day. But that night we found out that Fazlullah's men had switched off all the cable channels. They said that TV was *haram*; it showed the Westernized world, where women have love affairs and do not cover their hair. With nothing left to watch but the official government television channel, we were all but cut off from the outside world.

———————

Fazlullah, meanwhile, kept broadcasting his sermons. Girls should stay at home, he preached. We did our best to ignore him, until the day I came home to find my father with his head in his hands. "Oh, *jani*," he said, "the world has gone mad. Fazlullah and his men have blown up the girls' school in Matta."

My heart dropped. The school Fazlullah had destroyed was a primary school, not even a school that taught teenagers. He had bombed the school at night, when it was empty, but how cruel this man was, hurling firebombs at a place where little children wanted only to learn to read and write and add. Why? I wondered. Why was a school building such a threat to the Taliban?

I whispered a quick prayer for the children who'd lost their school and another to protect the Khushal School. *Please, God,* I prayed, *help us to protect our valley and to stop this violence.*

Every day, Fazlullah's men struck a new target. Stores, roads, bridges. And schools. Most of the attacks were outside Mingora, but soon they got closer. And closer. One day I was in the kitchen cleaning dishes—despite my best efforts to avoid them—and a bomb went off so close that the whole house rattled and the fan over the window fell. Before I could even react, the power went out. I learned that this was how it happened—bomb, then darkness. The Taliban bombed us, and then the power went out for an hour, at least.

A few days later, the Taliban struck again. A funeral for one of the victims of their last attack was being held in a nearby building. As the mourners gathered to pay their respects, a suicide bomber blasted himself. More than fifty-five people were killed, including members of Moniba's family.

I had grown up hearing the word *terrorism*, but I never really understood what it meant. Until now. Terrorism is different from war—where soldiers face one another in battle. Terrorism is fear all around you. It is going to sleep at night and not knowing what horrors the next day will bring. It is huddling with your family in the center-most room in your home because you've all decided it's the safest place to be. It is walking down your own street and not knowing whom you can trust. Terrorism is the fear that when your father walks out the door in the morning, he won't come back at night.

Now the enemy was everywhere and the attacks came out of nowhere. One day a store was destroyed. The next day, a house. Rumors flew. The store owner had crossed Fazlullah and had helped the army. The man whose house was targeted was a political activist. A bridge was blown up one day, a school the next. No place was safe. No one was safe.

Our family tried to carry on as normal, but we were tense all the time. Bombings became such a regular part of our daily lives that we fell into a routine every time we heard a blast. We called to one another to make sure everyone was safe. "*Khaista, pisho, bhabi*, Khushal, Atal!" we cried. Then we listened for the sirens. Then we prayed.

This kind of random terror made us do strange things. My father started taking a different route home each evening in case someone was studying his routine. My mother avoided the market, and my brothers stayed inside on even the sunniest days. And since I had been in the kitchen both times there were blasts near our house, I stayed as far from that room as possible. But how can a person live when she is afraid of a room in her own home? How can a mother buy food for her family if the market is a war zone? How can children gather for a game of cricket if a bomb could go off under their feet?

Nighttime was the worst. When darkness fell, we all startled at every creak and jumped at every shadow. Nighttime was when Fazlullah's men carried out most of their attacks—especially the destruction of schools. So every morning, before I rounded the corner on the way to the Khushal School, I closed my eyes and said a prayer—afraid to open them in case the school had been reduced to rubble overnight. This was what terrorism felt like.

In 2008 alone, the Taliban bombed two hundred schools. Suicide bombings and targeted killings were regular occurrences. Music shops closed, daughters and sisters were prevented from going to school, and during the month of Ramadan, we had no power or gas in Mingora because Fazlullah's men had blasted the electricity grid and the gas line.

One night, when a blast hit especially close to our home, I went to my father's side. "Are you scared now?" I asked.

"At night our fear is strong, *jani*," he said. "But in the morning, in the light, we find our courage again."

PART THREE

Finding My Voice

11

A Chance to Speak

Day or night, my father's courage never seemed to waver, despite receiving threatening letters as well as warnings from concerned friends. As the school bombings continued, he spoke out against them; he even went to the site of one school bombing while it was still a smoldering wreck. And he went back and forth to Islamabad and Peshawar, pleading with the government for help and speaking out against the Taliban.

I could see that my mother was worried at times. She would hug us close and pray over us before we left for school and as soon as we came home. And she sat late into the night with her phone in her hand—trying not to call my father every hour.

She talked to us of plans for what we would do if the Taliban came. She thought she could sleep with a knife under her pillow. I said I could sneak into the toilet and call the police. I thought of the magic pencil I used to pray for. Now would be as good a time as any for my prayer to finally be answered.

Back at school my friends and I wondered what we could do. So Madam Maryam and my father worked with us on essays and speeches in which we expressed our feelings about the Taliban's campaign to destroy girls' schools and about how much our own school meant to us. We planned an assembly where we would make our speeches; we called it a peace rally, but it was just going to be a handful of us upper-school girls.

The day of the assembly, a Pashto TV crew arrived at our school. We were excited and surprised—we didn't think anyone would care what a group of girls had to say about peace. Some girls were nervous, but I had given a few interviews by this time, and I was a bit more comfortable in front of a camera, although, truth be told, I did still get nervous.

We were a democracy at the Khushal School, so every girl would get a chance to speak. The older girls went first. They talked about our friends who had quit school out of fear. They talked about how much we loved to learn.

Then it was Moniba's turn. Moniba, our public-speaking champion, stepped to the front and spoke like a poet. "We Pashtuns are a religion-loving people," she said. "Because of the Taliban, the whole world is claiming we are terrorists. This is not the case. We are peace-loving. Our mountains, our trees, our flowers—everything in our valley is about peace."

After Moniba spoke, it was my turn. My mouth was as dry as dust. I was anxious, as I often was before interviews, but I knew this was an important opportunity to spread our message of peace and education. As soon as they put a microphone in front of me, the words came out—sure and steady, strong and proud. "This is not the Stone Age," I said. "But it feels like we are going backward. Girls are getting more deprived of our rights." I spoke about how much I loved school. About how important it was to keep learning. "We are afraid of no one, and we will continue our education. This is our dream." And I knew in that instant that it wasn't me, Malala, speaking; my voice was the voice of so many others who wanted to speak but couldn't.

Microphones made me feel as if I were speaking to the whole world. I had talked to only local TV stations and newspapers, but, still, I felt as if the wind would carry my words, the same way it scatters flower pollen in the spring, planting seeds all over the earth.

And I had started a funny habit: I sometimes found myself looking in the mirror and giving speeches.

Our house was often full of relatives from Shangla who came to Mingora when they needed to go to the doctor or do some shopping. The kitchen was full of aunties gossiping. The guest room was full of uncles arguing. And the house was full of little children playing. And crying. And arguing. With all this chaos swirling about, I would escape into the bathroom and look in the mirror. When I looked in the mirror, though, I didn't see myself. I saw hundreds of people listening to me.

My mother's voice would snap me out of my daydream.

"*Pisho*," she'd say. "What are you doing in there? Our guests need to use the bathroom."

I felt quite silly sometimes when I realized I was giving a speech to a mirror in the toilet. "Malala," I would say to myself, "what are you doing?"

Maybe, I thought, I was still that little Malala who lectured an empty classroom.

But maybe it was something more. Maybe that girl in the mirror, that girl who imagined speaking to the world, was the Malala I would become. So throughout 2008, as our Swat was being attacked, I didn't stay silent. I spoke to local and national TV channels, radio, and newspapers—I spoke out to anyone who would listen.

12

A Schoolgirl's Diary

"After the fifteenth of January, no girl, whether big or little, shall go to school. Otherwise, you know what we can do. And the parents and the school principal will be responsible."

That was the news that came over Radio Mullah in late December 2008. At first, I thought it was just one of his crazy pronouncements. It was the twenty-first century! How could one man stop more than fifty thousand girls from going to school?

I am a hopeful person—my friends may say too hopeful, maybe even a little crazy. But I simply did not believe that this man could stop us. School was our right.

We debated his edict in class. "Who will stop him?" the other girls said. "The Taliban have already blown up hundreds of schools, and no one has done anything."

"We will," I said. "We will call on our government to come and end this madness."

"The government?" one girl said. "The government can't even shut down Fazlullah's radio station!"

The debate went round and round. I didn't give in. But even to me, my argument sounded a bit thin.

One by one, girls stopped coming to school. Their fathers forbade them. Their brothers forbade them.

Within days we had gone from twenty-seven girls in our grade to ten.

I was sad and frustrated—but I also understood. In our culture, girls do not defy the males in their families. And I realized that the fathers and brothers and uncles who made my friends stay home were doing so out of concern for their safety. It was hard not to feel a bit depressed sometimes, not to feel as though the families who kept their girls at home were simply surrendering to Fazlullah. But whenever I'd catch myself giving in to a feeling of defeat, I'd have one of my talks with God. *Help us appreciate the school days that are left to us, God, and give us the courage to fight even harder for more.*

School had been due to end the first week of January for our usual winter break, so my father decided to postpone the holiday. We would remain in classes through 14 January. That way we could squeeze in every minute left to us. And the ten remaining girls in my class lingered in the courtyard every day after school in case these were our last chances to be together.

At home in the evenings I wondered what I would do with my life if I couldn't go to school. One of the girls at school had gotten married off before Fazlullah's edict. She was twelve. I knew my parents wouldn't do that to me, but I wondered, what *would* I do? Spend the rest of my life indoors, out of sight, with no TV to watch and no books to read? How would I complete my studies and become a doctor, which was my greatest hope at the time? I played with my shoebox dolls and thought: *The Taliban want to turn the girls of Pakistan into identical, lifeless dolls.*

While we girls savored the days until January 15, Fazlullah struck again and again. The previous year had been hard, but the days of January 2009 were among the darkest of our lives. Every morning, someone arrived at school with a story about another killing, sometimes two, sometimes three a night. Fazlullah's men killed a woman in Mingora because they said she was "doing *fahashi*," or being indecent, because she was a dancer. And they killed a man in the valley because he refused to wear his pants short the way the Taliban did. And now, we would be forbidden from going to school.

One afternoon I heard my father on the phone. "All the teachers have refused," he said. "They are too afraid. But I will see what I can do." He hung up and rushed out of the house.

A friend who worked at the BBC, the powerful British Broadcasting Corporation network, had asked him to find someone from the school to write a diary about life under the Taliban for its Urdu website—a teacher or an older student. All the teachers had said no, but Maryam's younger sister Ayesha, one of the older girls, had agreed.

The next day, we had a visitor: Ayesha's father. He would not allow his daughter to tell her story. "It's too risky," he said.

My father didn't argue with him. The Taliban were cruel; but even *they* wouldn't hurt a child, he wanted to say. But he respected Ayesha's father's decision and prepared to call the BBC with the bad news.

I was only eleven, but I said, "Why not me?" I knew he'd wanted someone older, not a child.

I looked at my father's hopeful—nervous—face. He had been so brave for speaking out. It was one thing to talk to national and local media, but this diary might be read by people outside Pakistan. It was the BBC, after all. My father had always stood by me. Could I stand by him? I knew without even thinking that I could. I would do anything to be able to continue going to school. But first we went to my mother.

If she was afraid, I wouldn't do it. Because if I didn't have her support, it would be like speaking with only half my heart.

But my mother agreed. She gave us her answer with a verse from the Holy Quran. "Falsehood has to die," she said. "And truth has to come forward." God would protect me, she said, because my mission was a good one.

Many people in Swat saw danger everywhere they looked. But our family didn't look at life that way. We saw possibility.

And we felt a responsibility to stand up for our homeland. My father and I are the starry-eyed ones. "Things have to get better," we always say. My mother is our rock. While our heads are in the sky, her feet are on the ground. But we all believed in hope. "Speaking up is the only way things will get better," she said.

I had never written a diary before and didn't know how to begin, so the BBC correspondent said he would help me. He had to call me on my mother's phone because, even though we had a computer, there were frequent power cuts and few places in Mingora with Internet access. The first time he called, he told me he was using his wife's phone because his own phone had been bugged by the intelligence services.

He suggested that I use a fake name so the Taliban wouldn't know who was writing the diary. I didn't want to change my name, but he was worried about my safety. That is why he chose a pseudonym for me: Gul Makai, which means "cornflower" and is the name of a heroine in a Pashtun folk story.

My first diary entry appeared on 3 January 2009, about two weeks before Fazlullah's deadline. The title was "I Am Afraid." I wrote about how hard it was to study or to sleep at night with the constant sounds of fighting in the hills outside town. And I described how I walked to school each morning, looking over my shoulder for fear I'd see a Talib following me.

I was writing from the privacy of my bedroom, using a secret identity, but thanks to the Internet, the story of what was happening in Swat was there for the whole world to see. It was as if God had at long last granted my wish for that magic pencil.

In my next entry, I wrote about how school was the center of my life and about how proud I was to walk the streets of Mingora in my school uniform.

As exciting as it was to be Gul Makai, it was hard not to tell anyone—especially at school. The diary of this anonymous Pakistani schoolgirl was all anyone talked about. One girl even printed it out and showed it to my father.

"It's very good," he said with a knowing smile.

———————

With the threat of school closing quickly becoming a reality, I appreciated going even more. In the days leading up to the last one, it was decided that wearing our uniforms was too danger-ous, so we were told to dress in our everyday clothes. I decided I wasn't going to cower in fear of Fazlullah's wrath. I would obey the instruction about the uniform, but that day I chose my brightest pink *shalwar kamiz*.

As soon as I left the house, I thought for a second about turning back. We'd heard stories of people throwing acid in the faces of girls in Afghanistan. It hadn't happened here yet, but with everything that *had* happened, it didn't seem impos-sible. But somehow my feet carried me forward, all the way to school.

What a peculiar place Mingora had become. Gunfire and

cannons as background noise. Hardly any people in the streets. (And if you did see anyone, you couldn't help but think, *This person could be a terrorist.*) And a girl in a pink *shalwar kamiz* sneaking off to school.

The BBC correspondent asked for more news from Swat for the next diary post. I didn't know what to tell him. He asked me to write about the killings. It seemed so obvious to him that this was news. But to me, what you experience every day is no longer news.

It was as if I had become immune to fear. Until one day, on my way home from school, I heard a man behind me say, "I will kill you." My heart stopped, but somehow my feet kept going. I quickened my pace until I was far ahead of him. I ran home, shut the door, and, after a few seconds, peeked out at him. There he was, oblivious to me, shouting at someone on his phone.

I laughed a bit at myself. "Malala," I told myself, "there are real things to be afraid of. You don't need to imagine danger where there is none."

The real worry, it seemed to me, was being found out. And, of course, it was Moniba who was first to guess the identity of Gul Makai. "I read a diary in the newspaper," she told me one day at recess, "and the story sounded like our story, what happens in our school. It's you, isn't it?" she said.

I could not lie, not to Moniba. But when I confessed, she became more angry than ever. "How can you say you're my best friend when you're keeping such an important secret from me?" She turned on her heel and left. And yet I knew, as angry as she was, she wouldn't reveal my secret.

It was my father who did that. By accident, of course. He was telling a reporter how terrifying it was for children just to walk to and from school. His own daughter, he said, thought a man on his phone had threatened to kill her. Just about everyone recognized the story from the diary, and by April, my days as Gul Makai, the secret diarist, would be over.

But the diary had done its job. Now a number of reporters were following the story of Fazlullah's attempt to shut down the girls' schools of Pakistan, including a man from the *New York Times*.

13

Class Dismissed

Ever since I'd started doing interviews, people in Mingora sometimes came up to me and told me I had done well. But many of my mother's friends were scandalized that I had shown my face on TV. Some even said that she would go to hell for not raising me better. And although my mother never said anything to me, I knew she would probably have preferred that I had worn a veil. But even if my mother disagreed with my choice—and even if her friends criticized her—she stood behind me.

Meanwhile, even some of my friends asked why I let the world see my face. "Fazlullah's men wear masks," I said, "because they are criminals. But I have nothing to hide, and I have done nothing wrong. I'm proud to be a voice speaking out for girls' education. And proud to show my identity."

A madman was about to kick more than fifty thousand

girls out of school in a matter of days, and all people seemed to want to talk about was whether I should have worn a veil! Meanwhile, my brother Khushal was saying that for once he wished he were a girl so he didn't have to go to school. I wondered sometimes if the world had turned upside down.

My mother and father liked to watch my interviews, but I usually ran out of the room when they came on the TV. I always liked to give interviews because I knew how important it was to speak for girls' rights, but I never liked to watch them. I don't know why. It was fine for the whole world to see me—I just didn't want to see myself!

And I suppose I have to admit that I'm a lot like all those people who were so preoccupied with my appearance. I suddenly noticed all kinds of things about my looks—things that had never much bothered me before. My skin was too dark. My eyebrows were too thick. One of my eyes was smaller than the other. And I hated the little moles that dotted my cheek.

A couple of days before the official school closing, my father was going to Peshawar to meet two video journalists from the *New York Times*, and I went with him. They had invited my father to ask if they could follow him on the last day of school, but at the end of the meeting, one of them turned to me and asked, "What would you do if there comes a day when you can't go back to your valley and school?" Because I was both stubborn and full of hope, I replied, "That will not happen." He insisted it might, and I started to weep. I think it was then that they decided to focus their documentary on me as well.

The morning of our last day at school, a two-man camera crew appeared at our house. I was still sleeping when they arrived. They told my father they were there to document my day—from start to finish. He was surprised; he had agreed to cameras in his school, not his home. I heard him try to talk the reporter out of this idea. Eventually he gave in and the filming began.

"They cannot stop me. I will get my education," I told the cameraman. "If it is in home, school, or anyplace. This is our request to the world—save our schools, save our Pakistan, save our Swat." I sounded hopeful, but in my heart, I was worried. As my father looked at me, smiling uncomfortably with a mixture of pride and sadness for his daughter, I pictured myself stuck at home, reading whatever books I could find until I ran out of books. I was eleven years old. Was my schooling really going to end now? Was I going to end up like girls who quit school to cook and clean? What I didn't know was that my words would reach many ears. Some in distant parts of the world. Some right in Swat, in Taliban strongholds.

Later, as my friends and I passed through the school gate and the video camera recorded our every move, it felt as if we were going to a funeral. Our dreams were dying.

Two-thirds of the students stayed home that day, even though we'd all vowed to be there for the last day. Then one of the girls burst through the doors. Her father and brothers had forbidden her from going to school, but as soon as they left for the day, she snuck out. What a strange world it was when a girl who wanted to go to school had to defy militants with machine guns—as well as her own family.

As the day went on, the teachers tried to act as if everything were normal. Some even gave us homework as if they'd be seeing us again after the winter vacation. Finally, the bell rang for the last time, and Madam Maryam announced it was the end of the term; but unlike in other years, no date was announced for the start of the next term. My friends and I all stood in the courtyard, hugging one another, too sad to leave.

Then we all made a decision. We would make our last day our best. We stayed late, just to make it last as long as possible. We went over to the elementary school building, where we'd all started as children, and played the games we'd played when we were little. Mango, Mango. Hopscotch. *Parpartuni.* We played silly games, sang nonsense rhymes—and pretended that, at least for those few hours, there was no Taliban.

Unfortunately on that day, Moniba was not talking to me, because we'd had a fight a few days earlier.

When I got home, I cried and cried. My mother cried, too. But when my father came home, he said, "Don't worry, *jani.* You will go to school."

But he was worried. The boys' school would reopen after the winter holiday, but the closing of the girls' school meant a significant loss of income, which he needed to pay teachers their salaries and the rents for the buildings. As usual, many of the families were behind in their tuition payments, and others had stopped paying when Fazlullah issued his edict. My father had spent the last few days before the holiday trying to find a way to pay the rents, the utility bills, and the teachers' salaries.

That night the air was full of artillery fire, and I woke up three times. The next morning, my family and I talked half-heartedly about leaving Swat or about sending me to a boarding school far away. But, as my father said, Swat was our home. We would stand by her in this time of trouble.

14

Secret School

My father wanted me to continue to improve my English. So he encouraged me to watch a DVD that one of the journalists in Islamabad had given me: a TV program called *Ugly Betty*.

I loved Betty, with her big braces and her big heart. I was in awe watching her and her friends as they walked freely down the streets of New York—with no veils covering their faces and no need for men to accompany them. My favorite part, though, was seeing Betty's father cook for *her* instead of vice versa!

But I learned another lesson watching the show. Although Betty and her friends had certain rights, women in the United States were still not completely equal; their images were used to sell things. In some ways, I decided, women are showpieces in American society, too.

When I watched, I looked at their hems cut so short and

their necklines so low, I wondered if there was a clothing shortage in the United States.

How crazy it was that this little plastic disc with images of a girl in big glasses and shiny braces was illegal. And how odd, too, to watch as Ugly Betty and her friends were free to walk the streets of New York City, while we were trapped inside with nothing to do.

Another show I was given was a British comedy from the 1970s. It's called *Mind Your Language* and about a classroom full of adults from all over the world trying to learn English. Madam Maryam gave it to my father, but I watched it, and it made me laugh and laugh. It's not good for learning English, though, because everyone on the show speaks it so poorly! But it's where I learned some of my favorite sayings, like "jolly good" and "h'okay" and "excooze me" and "thassalrye" (that's all right).

Meanwhile, my little brother Atal and his friends had started playing a new game. Instead of playing *parpartuni*, he and his friends were playing Army vs. Taliban. Children all over our neighborhood made pretend weapons out of whatever they could find. They fashioned guns out of sticks or folded paper, and grenades out of old water bottles.

War and terrorism had become child's play.

Sometimes my own little brothers—unaware of what it really meant—would pretend to be Taliban militants or army soldiers. They'd even set up bunkers on our roof, where they acted out a battle.

One day I saw Atal in the backyard furiously digging a hole.

"What are you doing?" I asked.

I shuddered when he gave me his answer in the most normal, natural tone of voice. "Making a grave," he said.

All the while, I kept up my blog posts as Gul Makai.

Four days after all girls' schools were shut down, Fazlullah's men destroyed five more schools. *I am quite surprised*, I wrote. *These schools had already been closed. Why did they also need to be destroyed?*

Meanwhile, the army was doing nothing about it but looking busy. Soldiers sat in their bunkers, smoking cigarettes, shelling all day, and firing cannons at the hills all night long. But in the mornings, the news would come not that the army had gained ground but that the Taliban had slaughtered two or three people. The people of Swat continued going to watch the floggings announced on Radio Mullah. And girls who only wanted to learn were trapped inside homes that had become like jails.

During those dark, dull days, we heard rumblings about secret talks with the Taliban. Then, out of nowhere, Fazlullah agreed to lift the ban on elementary school for girls. It was all right for little girls to go to school, he said, but he still insisted that girls over ten should stay home, in *purdah*.

I was eleven, but I wasn't going to let that stop me. Besides, I could easily pass as a ten-year-old.

Madam Maryam sent out a message to all the girls in the upper school: If they wanted to defy this new edict, she would open the school doors. "Just don't wear your uniforms," she said. "Dress in everyday clothes, plain *shalwar kamiz* that won't attract attention." So the next day, I put on everyday clothes and left home with my books hidden under my shawl and my head held high.

But Mingora had changed while school was closed for that month. Now the streets were ghostly quiet. Stores were shuttered, houses were dark, and even the normal din of traffic was a mere murmur. More than a third of the population had fled.

My friends and I were a little bit scared as we made our way to school on that first forbidden day, but we had a plan: If a Talib stopped us, we would just say, "We are in grade four."

———————

When I got to school that morning, I was more elated than ever to walk through the gate. Madam Maryam was waiting there for us, giving each girl a hug and telling us we were brave. She was brave, too, of course; she was taking a big risk being there. Girls like us might be reprimanded. A grown woman could be beaten. Or killed.

"This secret school," she said, "is our silent protest."

15

Peace?

One morning in February we awoke to gunfire. It wasn't un-usual for us to be awakened several times each night by the sounds of gunfire. But this was different.

The people of Mingora were firing guns into the air to celebrate a peace treaty. The government had agreed to impose *sharia* if the Taliban would stop fighting.

Sharia meant that all aspects of life—from property dis-putes to personal hygiene—would be dictated by religious judges. Even though people criticized the peace deal, I was happy because it meant I could go back to school.

Since 2007, more than a thousand people had been killed. Women had been kept in *purdah*, schools and bridges had been blown up, businesses had closed, and the people of Swat had lived with constant fear. But now it was all to stop. Perhaps the

Taliban would settle down, go back to their homes, and let us live as peaceful citizens.

Best of all, the Taliban had relented on the question of girls' schools. Even older girls could return to school. We would pay a small price, though; we could go to school as long as we kept ourselves covered in public. *Fine*, I thought, *if that's what it takes.*

While school was closed, I had continued doing interviews about girls' right to education, and my father and I attended rallies and events to spread our message as far and wide as we could. But now GEO TV, the biggest channel in our country, wanted to interview a girl about the peace treaty. We were being interviewed on the rooftop of a hotel at night. They wired me with a microphone and counted down: five-four-three-two-one.

The interviewer asked me how the peace deal would affect girls, and whether I thought it should happen. The peace treaty had only just been announced and already someone had violated it—a journalist who had recently interviewed my father had been killed.

I was disappointed in the treaty already, and I said so. "We are really sad the situation is getting worse. We were expecting peace and to go back to school. The future of our country can never be bright if we don't educate the young generation. The government should take action and help us."

But I wasn't done. I added, "I'm not afraid of anyone. I will get my education. Even if I have to sit on the floor to continue it. I have to continue my education, and I will do it."

How had I become so bold? I wondered. "Well, Malala," I told myself, "you're not doing anything wrong. You are speaking for peace, for your rights, for the rights of girls. That's not wrong. That's your duty."

After the interview, a friend of my father's asked him, "How old is Malala?"

When my father told him I was eleven, he was shocked. She is *pakha jenai*, he said, wise beyond her years.

Then he asked, "How did she get that way?"

My father said, "Circumstances have made her so."

———

But we were badly deceived. After the imposition of *sharia*, the Taliban became even bolder. Now they openly patrolled the streets of Mingora with guns and sticks as if they were the army. They killed policemen and dumped their bodies by the side of the road. They beat a shopkeeper because he allowed women to shop for lipstick unaccompanied. And they threatened the women at the bazaar, including my mother.

One day, when my mother went to the market to buy a gift for my cousin's wedding, a big, burly Talib accosted her and blocked her way. "I could beat you, you know, for leaving your home without the proper *burqa*," he said. "Do you understand?"

My mother was angry and frightened. He meant a shuttlecock *burqa*, which covers the whole face, with only a mesh grille to see through. She was wearing a fashion *burqa* and didn't even own the other kind. "Yes, okay," she said. "I will wear this in the future." She had never told a lie before. But, then again, she had never been confronted at the market by a man with a machine gun before.

"Good," said the man. "Next time, I will not be so nice to you."

Soon we learned that even a *burqa* was no protection against the whims of the Taliban.

One day I came home to find my father and his friends watching a video on his phone. I leaned in to see what the fuss was about. In the video, a teenage girl wearing a black *burqa* and red trousers was lying facedown on the ground being flogged in broad daylight by a bearded man in a black turban. "Please stop it!" she begged in between screams and whimpers as each blow was delivered. "In the name of Allah, I am dying!"

You could hear the Talib shouting, "Hold her down. Hold her hands down." At one point during the flogging, her *burqa* slipped up to reveal her trousers. The beating stopped for a moment so the men could cover her up again, then they went back to beating her. A crowd had gathered but did nothing. One of the girl's relatives even volunteered to help hold her down. By the time it was over, she had been struck thirty-four times.

A few days later the video was everywhere—even on TV— and the Taliban took credit. "This woman came out of her house with a man who was not her husband, so we had to punish her," a spokesman said. "Some boundaries cannot be crossed."

Woman? She was a teenager, maybe six years older than me. Yes, a boundary had been crossed. Grown men had taken to beating teenagers.

Soon the shelling began again. As we all huddled together in the dining room, one question was on our minds: What kind of peace was this?

The *New York Times* documentary had aired and brought even more attention to the plight of girls in Swat, and we started receiving messages of support from people all over the world. I saw then how powerful the media can be. We even heard from a nineteen-year-old Pakistani girl in the United States, a student at Stanford, Shiza Shahid. She would eventually play a big part in our campaign for education. For the first time, we knew our story was being heard beyond the borders of Pakistan.

On 20 April, Sufi Mohammad, the TNSM leader who had helped facilitate the peace deal between the government and the Taliban (and Fazlullah's father-in-law), came to Mingora to make a speech. That morning, my brothers and I peered out the gate as hundreds of people filed past our house on their way to the rally. Some teenage Taliban fighters went past, playing victory songs on their mobile phones and singing along in loud, excited voices. Quickly, we closed the gate so they couldn't see us. Eventually a huge crowd—nearly forty thousand people—gathered. And even though the field was quite a way from our house, we could hear the hum of thousands of voices chanting Taliban songs. It was a chilling sound.

Our father had left the house that morning to watch the rally from the rooftop of a nearby building. When he came home that evening, he looked as if he had aged a hundred years.

The speech was a disappointment. We had thought Sufi Mohammad would tell his followers to put down their weapons, but instead he called democracy un-Islamic and encouraged them to keep fighting. "It's not enough that they've had their way in Swat," my father said. "The Taliban are marching on Islamabad." Even some of Sufi Mohammad's own followers were unhappy with this turn of events.

Within days the Taliban streamed into the city of Buner, a town just south of Swat, only sixty miles from the capital. Now that the capital was at risk, the army planned a counterattack. Once again, Mingora was squarely in the middle.

This time, my mother said we should leave and take shelter in Shangla.

16

Displaced

"No Pashtun leaves his land of his own sweet will. Either he leaves from poverty or he leaves for love." So goes a famous Pashtun *tapa*, a couplet my grandmother taught me. Now we were being driven out by a force the writer could never have imagined—the Taliban.

I stood on our roof looking at the mountains, at the alleys where we used to play cricket, the apricot trees coming into bloom. I tried to memorize every detail in case I never saw my home again.

Then I went downstairs and tried to pack. It was chaos. My brothers were pleading with my mother to take their pet chicks with them, and my cousin's wife was in the kitchen crying. When I saw her crying, I started crying, too. My heart was full, but sometimes it's not until someone else cries that my tears feel free to flow. I ran into my room and tried to think about what I could take with me. I was traveling in Safina's family's car, so there wasn't much room. (The rest of my family was going in a car with my father's friend.) I packed my schoolbag first, with my books and papers. I took a last look at my trophies and said good-bye to them. Then I started stuffing clothes into a bag. In my haste, I took the pants from one set of *shalwar kamiz* and the top from another, so I ended up with things that didn't match.

When I closed the door to my room for possibly the last time and walked into the kitchen, I saw my mother telling Atal again that we couldn't take the chicks.

"What if they make a mess in the car?" she tried.

But Atal would not be swayed and suggested we buy them nappies to wear. Poor Atal. He was only five years old and already he'd known two wars in his short life. He was a child; the army and the Taliban were on a collision course with our home and all he cared about were his little birds. They couldn't go with us, of course, and when my mother said that they would have to stay behind with an extra ration of food and water, Atal burst into tears. Then, when she said I would have to leave my schoolbooks behind, I nearly cried, too. I loved school, and all I cared about were my books! We were children, after all, children with childish concerns, even with a war on the way.

I hid my books in a bag in our guest room, where it seemed safest, and whispered some Quranic verses over the books to protect them. Then the whole family gathered together and said good-bye to our house. We said some prayers and put our sweet home in God's protection.

Outside, the streets were choked with traffic. Cars and rickshaws, mule carts and trucks—all packed with people and their suitcases, bags of rice, and bedrolls. There were motorbikes with entire families balanced on them—and other people running down the street with just the clothes on their backs. Few people knew where they were going; they just knew they had to leave. Two million people were fleeing their homes. It was the biggest exodus in Pashtun history.

My mother and my brothers and I were going to stay with our family in Shangla. But our father said his duty was to go to Peshawar to warn people about what was going on. None of us liked this idea, especially my mother, but we understood. It was agreed that he would travel part of the way with us, then we would leave him in Peshawar.

The trip, which usually took a few hours, took two days. First we had to go out of our way because that's where Safina's family and my father's friend were going, and we were traveling with them in their cars because we didn't have one. When we got to the town of Mardan, we went on by ourselves, taking the Flying Coach as far as it would go. By the end of our journey, we were on foot. We had to walk the last fifteen miles on treacherous, washed-out roads, carrying all our things. It was nearly dark and a curfew would go into effect any minute when we reached the turnoff to Shangla. There, an army officer at a roadblock stopped us.

"Curfew. No one can pass through here," he said.

"We are IDPs," we told him. "We need to get to our family's village." But he still would not let us pass.

Internally displaced persons. That's what we were now, not Pakistanis, not Pashtuns. Our identity had been reduced to three letters: *IDP*.

We begged the man, and after my grandmother began to weep, he let us pass. As we walked those last few miles in the dark, shivers ran up and down our spines. We worried that an approaching army vehicle would mistake us for terrorists and shoot us in the back.

Finally, when we staggered into Shangla, our relatives were shocked. The Taliban had only recently left the mountains, but there was a rumor they would be back. "Why did you come here?" they asked.

For IDPs, there was no safe place.

———

We tried to settle into a new life in the mountains, not sure how long we'd be there. I signed up for the same class as my cousin Sumbul, who is a year older than me—and then realized I would have to borrow clothes from her because I had packed a mishmash of trousers and tunics.

It took us more than a half hour to walk to school, and when we arrived, I saw that there were only three girls in Sumbul's grade. Most of the village girls stop going to school after they turn ten, so the few girls who did go were taught alongside the boys. Meanwhile, I caused a bit of a shock because I didn't cover my face the way the other girls did and because I talked freely in class and asked questions.

I was soon to learn a lesson in country ways. It happened on the second day of school, when Sumbul and I arrived late for class. It was my fault—I always like to sleep in—and I started to explain. I was momentarily confused when the teacher told us to hold out our hands—then stunned when he slapped my and my cousin's palms with a stick.

I went to my seat, burning with humiliation. But after my embarrassment faded, I realized that this punishment meant I was simply being treated as one of the group.

I was content being with my cousins, but, oh, how I missed my home. And my old school. And my books. And even *Ugly Betty*.

The radio was our lifeline up in the mountains, and we listened to it constantly. One day in May the army announced that it had sent paratroopers into Mingora in preparation for a face-off with the Taliban there. A battle raged for four days—up and down the streets of Mingora. It was impossible to tell who was winning. And by the end, there was hand-to-hand combat in the streets.

I tried to picture it: Taliban men fighting in the alley where we played cricket. Army soldiers shooting out of hotel windows.

Finally, the army announced that it had the Taliban on the

run. It had destroyed Imam Deri, Fazlullah's stronghold. Then it captured the airport. Within four weeks, the army said it had taken back the city.

We breathed a little easier but wondered: Where would the Taliban go in retreat? Would they come back up here to the mountains?

———

All this time, we worried terribly about my father. It was nearly impossible to get a phone signal way up in the mountains, and sometimes my mother had to climb a big boulder in the middle of a field just to get one bar of service. So we almost never heard from him.

He was in Peshawar, staying in a room at a hostel with three other men, trying to get the media and the regional officials to understand what was going on in Swat this whole time. Then, after about two more weeks, he called and told us to join him in Peshawar.

We all wept with joy when we were finally reunited.

He had big news: Richard Holbrooke, a special ambassador from the United States, would be holding a meeting in Islamabad, and we were invited. But the morning of the meeting, we overslept! I hadn't set the alarm correctly, and my father was a bit angry with me. Somehow we made it to the hotel in time, though.

It was a conference of twenty social activists from war-stricken tribal areas across Pakistan, all gathered around a large table—and I was seated right next to the ambassador.

Mr. Holbrooke turned to look at me. "How old are you?" he said.

I straightened my posture to look as tall as possible. "I am twelve," I said. It was almost true; I would be twelve in a matter of days.

I took a deep breath. "Respected ambassador," I said. "I request you help us girls to get an education."

He laughed. "You already have lots of problems, and we are doing lots for you," he said. "We have pledged billions of dollars in economic aid; we are working with your government on providing electricity and gas, but your country faces a lot of problems."

I could not tell what his laughter meant. But I understood his words. The education of girls was far down on the list of issues that Pakistan faced. Maybe my posture sagged a little. Maybe my smile faded a bit. But I didn't really let on that I was disappointed. Besides, by now I knew: Just to get on TV and speak on behalf of girls' education was half the battle. The other half still lay ahead of us. And I would keep fighting.

After our visit to Islamabad, where we also held a press conference to share our story so that people would know what was happening in Swat, we didn't quite know where we would go next. Mingora was still smoldering. The Taliban were retreating into the mountains of Swat. So we accepted an invitation to stay in Abbottabad. Better yet was the news that Moniba was also staying in Abbottabad. She and I hadn't spoken since our fight just before the last day of school, but she was still my best friend.

So I called and invited her to meet me in a park; I took Pepsi and biscuits as a peace offering.

"It was all your fault," she told me.

I agreed. I didn't care who was right or wrong (although I'm pretty sure I had done nothing wrong). I was just happy to be friends again.

Meanwhile, my birthday was coming. All day I waited for the celebration—but in the chaos, everyone had forgotten. I tried not to feel sorry for myself, but I couldn't help thinking about how different my last birthday had been. I had shared a cake with my friends. There had been balloons, and I had made a wish for peace in our valley.

I closed my eyes and made that same wish on my twelfth birthday.

17

Home

After three months of living here and there, with strangers and relatives, we were finally on our way home. As we drove down the mountain pass and saw the Swat River, my father began to weep. And when we saw the condition of poor Mingora, we were all in tears.

Everywhere we looked, we saw buildings in rubble, piles of wreckage, burned-out cars, and smashed-out windows. Storefronts had had their heavy metal shutters pried off; their windows were gaping, their shelves empty. It seemed that every building was pockmarked with bullet holes.

It still felt like a war zone. Army soldiers peered down at us from machine-gun nests on the rooftops, their guns trained on the streets. And even though the government had said it was safe to go back, most people were still too afraid to return. The bus station, normally bustling with the chaos of brightly colored buses and hundreds of travelers, was deserted, and weeds were growing up through cracks in the paving.

But there was no sign of the Taliban.

As we rounded the corner to our home, we prepared ourselves for the worst. We had heard that the houses surrounding ours had been looted; TVs and jewelry had been stolen. We held our breath as our father unlocked the gate. The first thing we saw was that the garden in front of the house had become a jungle. My brothers immediately ran off to check on their pet chickens. They came back crying; all that was left was a pile of feathers and bones. Their birds had starved to death. Meanwhile, I ran to the guest room, where I had hidden my books. They were safe and sound. I said a prayer of thanks and paged through them. How lovely to see my quadratic equations, my social studies notes, and my English grammar book again.

I nearly wept for joy until I remembered: We still did not know whether our school had survived.

———

"Someone has been here," my father said as we entered the school gate.

The building across the street had been hit by a missile, but, miraculously, the school was intact. Inside, cigarette butts and food wrappers littered the floors. The chairs and desks were turned upside down in a jumble. The Khushal School sign was in the corner where my father had placed it for safekeeping. I lifted it up and screamed. Underneath were a handful of goats' heads. It took me a minute to realize that they were the remains of someone's dinner.

Anti-Taliban slogans were scribbled all over the walls. And inside the classrooms, bullet casings littered the floors. *"Army Zindabad!"*—which means "Long Live the Army"— was scrawled on a whiteboard. We understood, then, who'd been staying there. The soldiers had punched a hole in one of the walls on the upper floor, through which you could see the street below. Perhaps they had used this spot as a sniper's post. Although it was a mess, our beloved school was still standing.

After surveying the damage to the classrooms, my father and I went into his office. There he found a letter the army had left for him. It blamed the people of Swat for allowing the Taliban to take control of our homeland.

"We have lost so many of the precious lives of our soldiers— and this is due to your negligence," the letter said. "Long Live the Pakistani Army!"

My father shrugged. "How typical," he said. "First the people of Swat fall under the spell of the Taliban, then they are killed by the Taliban, and now they are blamed for the Taliban!"

It was all confusing. I used to want to become a doctor, but after everything we had been through, I began to think that becoming a political leader might be a better choice. Our country had so many problems. Maybe someday I could help solve them.

18

A Humble Request and a Strange Peace

Swat was finally at peace. The army remained, but the shops reopened, women walked freely in the markets—and I beat Malka-e-Noor for first place! I felt so hopeful about the future of my valley that I planted a mango seed outside our house. I knew it would take a long time for the seed to bear fruit, like the reconciliation and rebuilding the government had promised, but it was my way of saying I was full of hope for a long and peaceful future in Mingora.

One of my biggest worries in those days was that around the time I turned thirteen, I stopped growing. Whereas before, I was one of the tallest girls in my class, now I was among the smallest. So I had a humble request. Every night I prayed to Allah to make me taller, then I measured myself on my bedroom wall with a ruler and pencil. And every morning I would stand against it to check if I had grown. I even promised that if

I could grow just a tiny bit taller—even an inch—I would offer a hundred *raakat nafl*, extra prayers on top of my daily ones.

I was speaking at so many events, but I felt that my height got in the way of being authoritative. I was so short that sometimes it was hard to get people's attention!

In early 2010, our school was invited to take part in the District Child Assembly Swat, which had been set up by the charity UNICEF and by the Khpal Kor (My Home) Foundation for orphans. Sixty students from all over Swat had been chosen as members. They were mostly boys, but eleven girls from my school participated. And when we held an election for speaker, I won! It was strange to stand on a stage and have people address me as Madam Speaker, but I took the responsibility very seriously.

The assembly met almost every month for a year, and we passed nine resolutions. We called for an end to child labor. We asked for help to send disabled and street children to school. We demanded that all the schools that had been destroyed by the Taliban be rebuilt. Once the resolutions were agreed upon, they were sent to officials—and some were even acted on. We were being heard, we were making a difference, and it felt good.

By fall, clouds had gathered. A friend of my father's—a man who had spoken out against the Taliban—was ambushed on his way home. Then another man, a politician who had been critical of the Taliban, was killed by a suicide bomber. The summer of 2010 brought torrential rains—a monsoon that flooded the valley, sweeping away everything in its wake. Throughout Pakistan, more than two thousand people drowned, millions lost their homes, and seven thousand schools were destroyed.

Our home was on a bit of a rise, so we were safe from the flooding, but our school, on the banks of the river, was hit hard. When the waters receded, there were chest-high watermarks; our desks and chairs were covered with thick, foul-smelling mud. Repairs would be very costly. The damage in Shangla was even worse, and fundamentalist religious leaders suggested once again that God had sent a natural disaster as punishment for enjoying un-Islamic behaviors.

By early 2011, the Taliban had blown up two more schools. They kidnapped three foreign aid workers and murdered them. And another friend of my father's, a university president who'd been outspoken against the Taliban, was killed by two gunmen who burst into his office.

In May of that year, Osama bin Laden, the mastermind behind the 9/11 attacks, was killed in his hiding place in Abbottabad, just a stone's throw away from our military academy.

Then an anonymous letter addressed to my father came to our house. *You are the son of a religious cleric*, it said. *But you are like a convert. You are not a good Muslim. You have spoken against us, and you will face the consequences. The mujahideen will find you wherever you go on the surface of the earth.*

It was starting to seem as if the Taliban had never really left.

I tried to tell myself this terrible letter was just the futile and parting shot of a defeated Taliban. But, still, I prayed for my father's safety every day. I prayed for my school to remain open and for the bombed-out schools to be rebuilt. I also continued to ask God to make me taller. If I was going to become a politician and work for my country, I told God, I would have to at least be able to see over the podium.

19

Good News at Last

One day in October 2011 my father called me over to show me an e-mail he'd received. I could scarcely believe what it said: I had been nominated for the international peace prize of Kids Rights, a children's advocacy group based in Amsterdam. My name had been put forward by Archbishop Desmond Tutu from South Africa, one of my father's greatest heroes because of his fight against apartheid.

Then another e-mail arrived: I was invited to speak at a conference on education in Lahore. The chief minister there was starting a new network of schools; all the children would receive laptop computers. He was awarding cash prizes to children all over his province who did well in their exams. And to my surprise, he was also giving me an award for my campaign for girls' rights.

I wore my favorite pink *shalwar kamiz* to the event and

decided that I would tell everyone about how my friends and I in the girls' high school had defied the Taliban edict and continued going to school secretly. I wanted children everywhere to appreciate their education, so I said I now knew firsthand the suffering of millions of children who are deprived of an education. "But," I told the audience, "the girls of Swat were and are not afraid of anyone."

I had been home barely a week when one of my friends burst into class one day and announced that I'd won another prize. The government had awarded me Pakistan's first National Peace Prize. I couldn't believe it. So many journalists descended on our school that day it was a madhouse.

I still hadn't grown an inch by the date of the award ceremony, but I was determined to be seen as authoritative nonetheless. When the prime minister presented me with the award, I presented him with a list of demands—including a request that he rebuild the schools destroyed by Fazlullah and that the government establish a girls' university in Swat. That sealed my determination to become a politician—so I could take action and not just ask for help from others.

When it was announced that the prize would be awarded annually and be named the Malala Prize in my honor, I noticed a frown on my father's face. In our country's tradition, we don't honor people in this way while they are alive, only after they have died. He was a bit superstitious and thought it was a bad omen.

My brothers, of course, kept me humble. They still fought

with me and teased me and wrestled with me for the TV remote. I may have been getting attention from around the world, but I was still the same old Malala to them.

I wondered, though, how my friends would take to all this publicity. We were a very competitive group, after all. And, of course, there were always Moniba's feelings to consider. I worried that she'd think I'd abandoned her during my travels—or that she had taken up with a new best friend. But there was no time to think about this on my first day back at school. When I arrived, I was told there was a group of journalists waiting to interview me. When I entered the room, I saw all my school friends gathered round a cake, shouting, "Surprise!" They had taken up a collection and bought a white cake with chocolate icing that read SUCCESS FOREVER!

My dear friends, they were as generous as could be and only wanted to share in my success. I knew in my heart that any one of us could have achieved what I had; I was lucky that I had parents who encouraged me despite the fear we all felt.

"Now you can get back to your schoolwork," Madam Maryam said as we finished our cake. "Exams in March!"

PART FOUR

Targeted

20

A Death Threat against Me

One day in early 2012, we were in Karachi as guests of GEO TV, and a Pakistani journalist who lived in Alaska came to see us; she had seen the *New York Times* video and wanted to meet me. She also wanted to take my father aside to tell him something.

I noticed that she had tears in her eyes; then she and my father walked over to the computer. They looked troubled and hurriedly shut down whatever they'd been looking at.

A short while later, my father's phone rang. He took the call out of earshot and came back inside looking very gray. "What is it?" I asked. "There's something you're not telling me."

He had always treated me as an equal, but I could see he was trying to decide whether to protect me from this thing or to share it with me. He sighed heavily, then showed me what he'd been looking at on the computer.

He Googled my name. Malala Yousafzai, the Taliban said, "should be killed."

There it was in black and white. A death threat against me.

I think I had known this moment might come someday; now here it was. I thought back to those mornings in 2009, when school first reopened and I had to walk to school with my books hidden under my scarf. I was so nervous in those days. But I had changed since then. I was three years older now. I had traveled and given speeches and won awards. Here was a call for my death—an invitation from one terrorist to another, saying, "Go ahead, shoot her"—and I was as calm as could be. It was as if I were reading about someone else.

I took another glance at the message on the screen. Then I closed the computer and never looked at those words again. The worst had happened. I had been targeted by the Taliban. Now I would get back to doing what I was meant to do.

I might have been calm, but my dear father was near tears. "Are you all right, *jani*?" he said.

"*Aba*," I said, trying to reassure him. "Everybody knows they will die someday. No one can stop death. It doesn't matter if it comes from a Talib or from cancer."

He wasn't convinced. "Maybe we should stop our campaigning for a while," he said. "Maybe we should go into hibernation for a time." My proud, fearless Pashtun father was shaken in a way I'd never seen. And I knew why. It was one thing for him to be a target of the Taliban. He had always said,

"Let them kill me. I will die for what I believe in." But he had never imagined the Taliban would turn their wrath on a child. On me.

I looked at my father's wretched face, and I knew that he would honor my wishes no matter what I decided. But there was no decision to make. This was my calling. Some powerful force had come to dwell inside me, something bigger and stronger than me, and it had made me fearless. Now it was up to me to give my father a dose of the courage he had always given me.

"*Aba*," I said. "You were the one who said if we believe in something greater than our lives, then our voices will only multiply, even if we are dead. We can't stop now."

He understood, but he said we should be careful about what we say and to whom we say it.

On the trip back home, though, I asked myself what I would do if a Talib came to kill me.

Well, I would just take my shoe and hit him.

But then I thought: *If you hit a Talib with your shoe, there is no difference between him and you. You must not treat others with cruelty. You must fight them with peace and dialogue.*

"Malala," I said to myself. "Just tell him what is in your heart. That you want an education. For yourself. For all girls. For his sister, his daughter. For him."

That's what I would do. Then I would say, "Now you can do what you want."

21

The Promise of Spring

By spring the valley had begun to warm, the poplar trees had burst into bloom, and a tiny miracle in the campaign for education had taken place right in my own home. My mother had started learning to read.

While my father and I were busy crisscrossing Swat, speaking out on behalf of the girls of our valley, my mother had started working with one of the teachers at the Khushal primary school. Whenever Miss Ulfat had a break in her schedule, my mother would visit, her notebook and pencil in hand, until gradually the strange squiggles and symbols on the page revealed themselves to her. She was soon able to read Urdu— and had started learning English.

My mother loved schoolwork even more than I did, if that was possible. My father said it was because she had been deprived of learning for so long. In the evenings, she and I would often do our homework together, sipping tea—two generations of Pashtun women happily huddled over their books.

Meanwhile, my own schoolwork had actually slipped a bit because of all my travels. I could hardly believe it, but Malka-e-Noor had come in first the previous term. And, of course, Khushal seized the opportunity to tease me. "While you were busy becoming the most famous student in Pakistan, your rival stole your crown at home!" he said.

But it hardly mattered. My friends and I were in high spirits because exams were finally over and our class was about to go on our first field trip in years. During Fazlullah's reign, all field trips had been canceled since girls were not to be seen in public. Now, finally, our beloved springtime ritual was back.

We traveled by bus to the famous White Palace, a wonder built of white marble so unearthly it floated like a cloud. My friends and I stared in awe at its rooms and gardens. Then we ran around, chasing one another, in the deep green forest. When we came upon a crystal waterfall, we all posed for pictures.

One girl splashed another. The drops of water lit the air like diamonds. It was one of the most beautiful things I'd ever seen, and we all sat dreamily for a while, just listening to the rushing water.

Then Moniba started splashing me again. I wasn't in the mood, so I told her to stop. But she did it again. And again. My father called for me, so I walked off. When I returned, she was angry with me for walking away. And once again, our typical foolishness put a damper on the day. We rode home in the bus, sulking in our separate seats.

The next morning, a man came to our door with a photocopied letter. As my father read it to us, the color drained from his face.

Dear Muslim brothers,
There is a school, the Khushal School…which is
a centre of vulgarity and obscenity. They take girls for
picnics to different resorts. Go and ask the manager of
the White Palace Hotel and he will tell you what these
girls did.…

He put down the piece of paper. "It has no signature," he said. We sat stunned. We knew nothing improper had happened on our field trip.

Our phone began to ring. The letters, apparently, had been distributed all over the neighborhood and pasted on the walls of the mosque near our school.

It was clear to us now that someone had spied on us during our school trip.

And someone had gone to a lot of trouble to spread lies about us and our school. There was no denying it: The Taliban might have been defeated, but their beliefs were still spreading.

22

Omens

That summer I turned fifteen. Many girls are married off by that age. And many boys have already left school to support their families. I was lucky. I would get to stay in school as long as I wanted. And as long as there was peace—well, relative peace. The bomb blasts were down to only two or three a year, and you could pass by the Green Square without seeing the aftermath of a Taliban killing spree. But true peace seemed like nothing more than a memory, or a hope.

This birthday felt like a turning point for me. I was already considered an adult—that happens at age fourteen in our society. But it was time for me to take stock, to think about my future. I knew for certain now that I wanted to be a political leader. I felt the word *politics* had a bit of a stain on it, but I would be different. I would do the things politicians only spoke of. And I would start with education—especially girls' education. Just because I no longer had to fight to go to school didn't mean I had any less interest in the cause.

I had been given a lot of awards, and I started to feel that it was too much. That I didn't deserve it all. I saw so many children suffering still—why should I be enjoying galas and ceremonies? I told my father I wanted to spend some of the money I'd received helping people who needed it. I had never forgotten the children I'd seen sorting trash at the dump all those years earlier. I wanted to help kids like them. So I decided to start an education foundation. I organized a meeting with twenty-one girls at school, and we discussed how we could help every girl in Swat get an education. We decided we would focus on street children and those in child labor. We had plans to keep talking, and then in the fall, we would decide what exactly we could do.

In early August my father received some frightening news. One of his close friends, Zahid Khan, had been attacked. Like my father, he was an outspoken opponent of the Taliban. On his way home from prayers one night, he was shot—point-blank in the face.

When my father got the news, he fell to his knees; it was as if *he* had been shot.

"We were both on the Taliban list," he finally confessed to my mother. "People were just wondering which of us would be first."

Although we had been told that the Taliban had fled, there was still violence in the valley. Whereas before, anyone in the region who happened to be caught in the crossfire was in danger, now the threat was mostly to those who had spoken against the Taliban in the past and who were continuing to campaign for peace.

By some miracle, Zahid Khan survived. After that, though, I noticed a change in my father. He started to vary his routine each day. One day he would go to the primary school first thing in the morning; another day he would go to the girls' school, and the next to the boys'. And before he stepped inside, he looked up and down the street four or five times to be sure he wasn't being followed.

At night he would come to my room pretending he was there to say good night. But he was actually checking to make sure all my windows were locked. I knew what he was doing, so I'd say, "*Aba*, why have you closed the windows?"

He'd reply, "*Jani*, I've closed the windows because I want you to be safe!"

"If the Taliban had wanted to kill me," I told him, "they should have done it in 2009. That was their time."

He would shake his head at me and say, "No, you should be safe."

My room was big and at the front of the house, and it had many windows. I did worry sometimes that a person could climb over the boundary wall and jump into my room. I also worried constantly that someone had forgotten to lock the gate. So after the rest of the family was asleep, I would tiptoe outside and check the lock.

All that fall, odd things happened. Strangers came to the house asking my father questions about his friends and his family. My father told me they were from the intelligence services. Sometimes they came to the school and snooped around.

There were little things, too. A teacher came to school hysterical one morning, saying she had had a nightmare about me. "You were badly hurt," the teacher said. "Your legs were on fire." And a picture of me that hung on a wall in our house mysteriously shifted overnight. My father, the gentlest man I know, was very upset when he discovered it hanging crooked the next morning. "Please put it straight!" he snapped at my mother.

I had started having nightmares, too. Dreams where men threw acid in my face. Dreams where men snuck up behind me. Sometimes I thought I heard footsteps echoing mine when I turned down the alley in front of our house. And sometimes I imagined figures slipping into the shadows when I passed.

I had also started thinking about death, wondering what it felt like.

I didn't tell my parents about my dreams and fears, or even Moniba. I didn't want anyone to worry.

23

A Day Like Any Other

The second Tuesday in October started out the same as any other. I was late, as usual, because I'd slept in, as usual. I'd stayed up extra late after talking to Moniba, studying for my year-end exam in Pakistani studies. I'd already done a disappointing job on my physics exam, so I would have to get a perfect score on this exam if I was going to take the number one spot back from Malka-e-Noor. It was a point of pride. It was also a sibling thing: If I didn't come in first, I'd never hear the end of it from Khushal.

I gulped down a bit of fried egg and chapati with my tea and raced out the door, just in time to catch the bus crammed with other girls on their way to school. I was happy that morning, ridiculously happy. Before I left, my father had been teasing Atal, saying he could be my secretary when I became prime minister. And of course, Atal said, no, he would be prime minister, and I would be *his* secretary.

It seemed as if everything in my life was going well. My mother was learning to read. I was on my way to the school I loved. And Moniba and I were friends again. I told myself not to worry about Malka-e-Noor and instead to work hard. And, I thought, I should thank God for all I had. So I did. I whispered a prayer of thanks before I managed a few last minutes of studying for my exam. *Oh, and God,* I said, *please don't forget to give me first place, since I have worked so hard.*

I always prayed the most during exams. Usually, I did not pray "on time," which means praying five times a day, our religious duty. But at this time of year, my friends and I all prayed on time. I asked for help with my exams, or help to come in first in the class. Our teachers always told us, though, "God won't give you marks if you don't work hard. God showers us with his blessings, but he is honest as well." So I always worked hard, too.

––––––

Exam morning passed, and I felt confident I had done well. Afterward, Moniba suggested that we stay behind and wait for the second pickup, which we did often so we could chat before going home.

When the *dyna* arrived, I looked around for Atal. My mother had told him to ride home with me that day.

But soon I was distracted as the girls gathered around to

watch our driver do a magic trick with a disappearing pebble. No matter how hard we tried, we could not figure out his secret. I forgot all about Atal as we piled into the van. We squeezed in and took our usual places, about twenty girls in all. Moniba was next to me, and the rest of my friends were across from us on the other bench. A little girl named Hina grabbed the seat next to me, the spot where my friend Shazia usually sat—forcing Shazia to sit on the bench in the middle, where we often put our backpacks. Shazia looked so unhappy, I asked Hina to move.

Just as the van was about to pull away, Atal came running. The doors were shut, but he jumped onto the tailboard on the back. This was a new trick of his, riding home, hanging off the tailboard. It was dangerous, and our bus driver had had enough of it.

"Sit inside, Atal," he said.

But Atal didn't budge.

"Sit inside with the girls, Atal Khan Yousafzai, or I won't take you!" the driver said, with more force this time.

Atal yelled that he would rather walk home than sit with girls. He jumped down and stormed off in a huff.

It was hot and sticky inside the *dyna* as we bounced along Mingora's crowded rush-hour streets, and one of the girls started a song to pass the time. The air was thick with the familiar smell of diesel, bread, and kebab mixed with the stench from the nearby stream, where everyone dumped trash. We turned off the main road at the army checkpoint as always and passed the poster that read WANTED TERRORISTS.

Just after we passed the Little Giants snack factory, the road became oddly quiet and the bus slowed to a halt. I don't remember a young man stopping us and asking the driver if this was the Khushal School bus. I don't remember the other man jumping onto the tailboard and leaning into the back, where we were all sitting. I never heard him ask, "Who is Malala?" And I didn't hear the *crack, crack, crack* of the three bullets.

The last thing I remember is thinking about my exam the next day. After that, everything went black.

PART FIVE

A New Life, Far from Home

24

A Place Called Birmingham

I woke up on 16 October to a lot of people standing around looking at me. They all had four eyes, two noses, and two mouths. I blinked, but it did no good. I was seeing everything in double.

The first thing I thought was *Thank God, I'm not dead.*

But I had no idea where I was or who these people were.

They were speaking English, although they all seemed to be from different countries. I tried to talk, since I could speak English, but no sound came out. There seemed to be a tube of some kind in my throat, a tube that had stolen my voice.

I was in a high bed, and all around me, complicated machines beeped and purred. I understood then. I was in a hospital.

My heart clenched in panic. If I was in a hospital, where were my parents? Was my father hurt? Was he alive? Something had happened to me, I knew. But I was sure something had happened to my father as well.

A nice woman wearing a headscarf came to my side. She told me that her name was Rehanah and that she was the Muslim chaplain. She began to pray in Urdu. Instantly I felt calm, comforted, and safe. As I listened to the beautiful, soothing words of the Holy Quran, I closed my eyes and drifted off.

When I opened my eyes next, I saw that I was in a green room with no windows and very bright lights. The nice Muslim woman was gone; a doctor and a nurse were in her place.

The doctor spoke to me in Urdu. His voice was oddly muffled, as if he were speaking from a great distance. He told me that I was safe and that he had brought me from Pakistan. I tried to talk but couldn't, so I tried to trace letters on my hand, thinking I could spell out a question. The nurse left and came back with a piece of paper and a pen for me, but I couldn't write properly. I wanted to give them my father's number, I wanted to write a question, but everything came out all jumbled. So the nurse wrote the alphabet on a piece of paper and I pointed at letters.

The first word I spelled out was *father*. Then *country*.

Where was my father? I wanted to know. And what country was this?

The doctor's voice was still hard to hear, but he seemed to

be saying I was in a place called Birmingham. I didn't know where that was. Only later did I figure out it was in England.

He hadn't said anything about my father. Why not? Something had happened to him. That was the only reason there could be. I had it in my head that this doctor had found me on the roadside and that he didn't know my father was also hurt. Or that he didn't know how to find my father. I wanted to give him my father's phone number so he could tell him, "Your daughter is here."

I moved ever so slightly to spell out *father* again, and a blinding pain cut through my head. It was as if a hundred razors were inside my skull, clattering and rattling around. I tried to breathe. Then the nurse leaned down and dabbed at my left ear with a piece of gauze, and blood came away on the cloth. My ear was bleeding. What did that mean? I tried to lift my hand to touch it, but I noticed, as if from a distance, that my hand did not seem to be working properly. What had happened to me?

Nurses and doctors came in and out. No one told me anything. Instead, they asked me questions. I nodded and shook my head in reply. They asked if I knew my name. I nodded. They asked if I could move my left hand. I shook my head. They had so many questions, and yet they wouldn't answer mine.

It was all too much. The questions, the pain in my head, the worry about my father. When I closed my eyes, I didn't see darkness, only a bright light, as if the sun were shining under my eyelids. I was fading in and out, but I never felt as if I had slept. There was only the long stretches of being awake, my head filled with pain and questions, and then not.

The room I was in was in the ICU and didn't have windows, so I never knew if it was day or night. I knew only that no one had answered my constant question: Where was my father?

But eventually a new question joined it when I looked around the room at all the complicated medical equipment: Who would pay for this?

A lady walked in and told me her name was Dr. Fiona Reynolds. She spoke to me as if we were old friends. She handed me a green teddy bear—which I thought was an odd color for it—and a pink notebook. The first thing I wrote was *Thank you.*

Then I wrote, *Why I have no father?*

And *My father has no money. Who will pay for this?*

"Your father is safe," she said. "He is in Pakistan. Don't worry about the payment."

If my father was safe, why wasn't he here? And where was my mother?

I had more questions for Dr. Fiona, but the words I needed would not come to my mind. She seemed to understand. "Something bad happened to you," she said. "But you're safe now."

What had happened? I tried to remember. All sorts of images floated through my head. I didn't know what was real and what was a dream.

I am on a bus with my father, and two men shoot us.

I see a crowd gathered around me as I lie on a bed, or maybe a stretcher. I can't see my father, and I'm trying to cry out, *Where is* aba, *where is my father?* But I can't speak. And then I see him and I feel joy and relief.

I feel someone hovering over me, a man, whose hands are poised above my neck, ready to choke me.

I am on a stretcher, and my father is reaching out to me.

I am trying to wake up, to go to school, but I can't. Then I see my school and my friends and I can't reach them.

I see a man in black pointing a gun at me.

I see doctors trying to stick a tube in my throat.

I am telling myself, *You are dead.* But then I realize that the angel has not yet come to ask the questions a Muslim hears after death: *Who is your God? Who is your prophet?* I realize then I can't be dead, and I fight and struggle and kick and try to wake from this terrible nightmare.

These images seemed very real, yet I knew they couldn't all be. But somehow I had ended up in this place called Birmingham, in a room full of machines, with only the green teddy bear at my side.

25

Problems, Solutions

In those first days of being in the hospital, my mind drifted in and out of a dreamworld. I thought I had been shot, but I wasn't sure—were those dreams or memories?

I couldn't remember words, either. I wrote to the nurses asking for a *wire to clean my teeth*. I had a pounding, nonstop headache; I was seeing double; I could hardly hear; I couldn't move my left arm or close my left eye—but for some reason all I wanted to do was floss my teeth.

"Your teeth are fine," the doctors said. "But your tongue has gone numb." I tried to shake my head. No, I wanted to explain, there was something stuck in my teeth. But shaking my head set off the razor-blade pain, so I held still. I couldn't convince them. And they couldn't convince me.

Then I saw that my green teddy bear was gone. A white one

had taken its place. I felt a special affection for the green teddy bear, since he was by my side that first day; he helped me.

I took the notebook and wrote, *Where's the green teddy?*

No one gave me the answer I wanted. They said it was the same teddy that had been by my side the first day. The lights and walls had given him a green glow, but the teddy was white, they said. He was always white.

Meanwhile, the bright lights in my room were excruciating, like hot white daggers to my eyes, especially my poor left eye, which wouldn't close. *Stop lights*, I begged in my notebook.

The nurses did their best to darken the room, but as soon as I got some relief from the pain, my thoughts circled back to my father. *My father?* I wrote again in the notebook. When you can't move, you can't hear, and you can't see properly, your mind spins and spins—and my mind kept going back to the same question. Where was my father?

———

Every time a different doctor or nurse came into my room to change my blanket or check my eyesight, I handed them the notebook and pointed to the questions about my father. They all said not to worry.

But I did worry. I couldn't stop.

I was also obsessed with how we would pay for all this. Whenever I saw the doctors and nurses talking to each other,

I thought for sure that they were saying, "Malala doesn't have any money. Malala can't pay for her treatment." There was one doctor who always looked sad, so I wrote him a note. *Why are you sad?* I asked. I thought it was because he knew I couldn't pay. But he replied, "I'm not sad."

Who will pay? I wrote. *We don't have any money.*

"Don't worry. Your government will pay," he said. After that, he always smiled when he saw me.

Then a new worry seized me. Did my parents know where *I* was? Maybe they were wandering the streets and alleys of Mingora looking for me. But I am a hopeful person, and therefore when I see problems, I will always think about solutions. So I thought I would go to the hospital's reception desk and ask for a phone so I could call my parents.

But then I realized I didn't have the money to pay for such an expensive call. I didn't even know how to dial Pakistan from here. Then I thought, *I need to go out and start working to earn money so I can buy a phone and call my family so we can all be together again.*

Dr. Fiona came into my room and handed me a newspaper clipping. It was a picture of my father standing next to the Pakistan army's chief of staff. My father was alive! And in the background of the photo was Atal!

I smiled. Something bad had happened to me. But I was alive and now I knew my father was alive. That was a reason to be thankful.

Then I noticed a figure in a shawl sitting in the back of the photo near my brother. I could just make out her feet. Those were my mother's feet!

That's my mother! I wrote to Dr. Fiona.

That night I slept a bit better. It was a sleep full of strange dreams. Dreams of being on a bed surrounded by lots of people. Dreams of being shot. Dreams of a bomb exploding. I would wake up and look around for the green teddy. But always it was just the white one.

Now that I knew my family was safe, I spent all my time worrying about how we would pay for my treatment. Obviously, my father was at home because he was selling our few possessions to pay for all this. Our house was rented; the school building was, too. Even if he sold everything we owned, it would never be enough. Was he borrowing money? Was he calling on his friends to ask for a loan?

Later that day, the man who had spoken to me in Urdu, Dr. Javid Kayani, came in with his cell phone. "We're going to call your parents," he said matter-of-factly.

I couldn't believe it.

"You won't cry," he said firmly. "You won't weep. You will be strong. We don't want your family to worry."

I nodded. I hadn't cried once since I'd arrived. My left

eye was constantly weeping, but I had not cried.

After a series of blips and beeps, I heard my father's dear and familiar voice. "*Jani?*" he said. "How are you feeling, my *jani?*"

I couldn't reply because of the tube in my throat. And I couldn't smile because my face was numb. But I was smiling inside, and I knew my father knew that.

"I'll come soon," my father said. "Now have a rest, and in two days we will be there."

His voice was loud and bright. Maybe a little too bright.

Then I realized: He had also been told not to cry.

26

A Hundred Questions

I wrote a new note in my pink diary. *Mirror.*

When I got my wish and the nurses brought me a small white mirror, I was surprised at what I saw. Half of my head was shaved and my long hair was gone. Stitches dotted my left brow. A huge purple and yellow bruise surrounded my left eye. My face was swollen to the size of a melon. And the left corner of my mouth turned down in a frown.

Who was this poor, distorted Malala? And what had happened to her?

I was confused, but I wasn't upset. Just curious. And I didn't know how to express what I was feeling.

Now my hair is small was all I could write.

Had the Taliban shaved my head? I wondered.

Hwo did this to me? I wrote, my letters scrambled. *What happened to me?*

Dr. Fiona said what she always said. "Something bad happened to you, but you are safe."

But this time it wasn't enough. I pointed at my words.

Was I shot? I wrote. I couldn't move the pencil fast enough to keep up with my questions. Had anyone else been hurt? I wondered. Had there been a bomb?

I was getting frustrated with my sore head and my bad memory and the tube that prevented me from talking. I started to squirm. I would get out of here and find a computer so I could check my e-mail and ask someone what happened. I saw the cell phone on Dr. Fiona's belt and signaled to her that I wanted it—I mimed dialing on my palm, then brought the "phone" to my ear.

Dr. Fiona placed a gentle hand on my wrist and sighed. Then she spoke very slowly and calmly. "You were shot," she said. "On the bus, on your way home from school."

So they did it, I thought. The Taliban really did what they said they would do. I was furious. Not that they'd shot me. That I hadn't had a chance to talk to them. Now they'd never hear what I had to say.

"Two other girls were hurt," Dr. Fiona said. "But they're all right. Shazia and Kainat."

I didn't recognize these names. Or if I did, I couldn't remember who these girls were.

She explained that the bullet had grazed my temple, near my left eye, and traveled eighteen inches down to my left shoulder, where it stopped. It could have taken out my eye or gone into my brain, she said. "It's a miracle you're alive."

I tried to speak but remembered I couldn't.

I took the mirror and pointed to a splatter of black dots near my temple.

Dr. Fiona grimaced slightly. "Gunpowder." I lifted my hand and showed her more black dots on the fingers of my left hand. "That's gunpowder, too," she said. "You must have lifted your hand to cover your face at the last minute."

I will admit that I used to be sensitive about my looks. I was never satisfied. My nose was too big. I had funny black spots on my face. My skin was too dark. Even my toes were too long.

But I looked at this Malala in the mirror with nothing but curiosity. I was like a scientist studying a specimen. I wanted to understand exactly what had happened, where the bullet went, what exactly it had done. I was fascinated by what I saw.

I wasn't sad. I wasn't scared. I just thought: *It doesn't matter what I look like. I am alive. I was thankful.*

I glanced over at Dr. Fiona. She had positioned a box of tissues between us, and I realized then that she'd been expecting me to cry. Maybe the old Malala would have cried. But when you've nearly lost your life, a funny face in the mirror is simply proof that you are still here on this earth. I just wanted to learn more about what the bullet had done. Had it passed through my brain? Was that why I couldn't hear properly? Why couldn't I shut my left eye? And what does any of this have to do with what's going on with my left arm?

I had a hundred questions for Dr. Fiona, but I only asked one. *How soon can I go home?*

27

Passing the Hours

One day another Fiona came to my room. Her name was Fiona Alexander, and she said she was the head of communications for the hospital. I thought this was funny; I couldn't imagine the hospital in Swat having a communications office.

She said the hospital would like to take a picture of me. I thought *this* was really funny. Why would anyone want a photo of me looking the way I did?

Would it be okay to take my picture? Fiona asked again. I didn't see the point of a picture of me with my swollen face in a hospital bed, but everyone here was so nice, and I wanted to be nice in return. And I thought maybe my parents would see a picture of me and this would give them hope and bring them to me faster. I agreed, but I made two demands: I asked for a shawl so I could cover my hair, and I asked her to please take the picture from my right side. The left side of my face still would not cooperate.

———

The worst thing about being in the hospital was the boredom. While I waited for my family, I stared at the clock in my room. The movement of the hands around the dial reassured me that I was, indeed, alive and helped me measure off the minutes until my family arrived. The clock had always been my enemy at home—stealing my sleep in the morning when all I wanted to do was hide under the blanket. I couldn't wait to tell my family that I had finally made friends with the clock—and for the first time in my life I was waking up early! Every morning, I waited eagerly for 7:00 AM, when friends like Yma, who worked at the hospital, and nurses from the children's hospital would come and help me pass the hours.

When I could see well enough, they brought me a DVD player and a stack of DVDs.

During my first days, they had turned on the TV for me—I watched the BBC for a few minutes and they were talking about the American elections between President Barack Obama and that other man, and then they changed the channel to *MasterChef*, which I had watched back in Pakistan—but my vision was still so blurry then that I asked them to turn it off and didn't ask to watch TV again.

But now my eyesight was better, although I was still seeing

double a bit. I got to choose from *Bend It Like Beckham, High School Musical, Hannah Montana,* and *Shrek.* I chose *Shrek.* I loved it so much I watched the sequel right after.

One of the nurses figured out that if she covered my damaged eye with a cotton patch, my double vision wasn't as bad. Meanwhile, my left ear kept bleeding and my head kept throbbing. But I passed the day with a green ogre and a talking donkey while I waited for my parents to come to England.

On the fifth day, the tube in my throat was removed, and I got my voice back. It was around this time that I put my hand on my tummy and felt something odd. There was a hard lump just under the skin. "What is this?" I asked one of the nurses.

"It's the top of your skull," she said.

I was sure I'd misunderstood. Between my bad hearing and my trouble with words, I thought she'd said the top of my skull was in my tummy!

Dr. Fiona arrived to explain. When the bullet hit my temple, it fractured the bone, sending splinters of bone into the lining of my brain. The shock caused my brain to swell. So the doctors in Pakistan removed a piece of my skull to allow the brain to expand. To keep the bone safe, they placed it under the skin of my abdomen.

I had lots of questions for Dr. Fiona; it was like being back in biology class at school. I wanted to know exactly how they removed my skull. With a saw, Dr. Fiona replied. What happened after that? I asked.

Dr. Fiona explained that the surgery had been a success but that I had developed an infection and that my condition had started to worsen. My kidneys and lungs began to fail, and soon I was near death. So the doctors put me in a coma; that way I could fly to England for better care.

"You flew in a private jet," she said.

"A private jet? How do you know?" I asked.

"Because I was on the flight with you," she said.

I later learned that the United Arab Emirates had offered the plane, which was fully equipped with an onboard medical unit.

Dr. Fiona explained that she and Dr. Javid had been in Pakistan advising army doctors on how to set up a liver-transplant system. Dr. Javid was contacted for his advice, and he brought Dr. Fiona with him since she was a specialist in children's emergency care. She admitted she had been a little nervous about flying into Peshawar, because it had become dangerous for foreigners. But when she found out I was a campaigner for girls' rights, she came.

She and Dr. Javid told the doctors in Pakistan that I wouldn't survive unless I was moved to a better-equipped hospital, so my parents agreed to let me go with them. Dr. Fiona and Dr. Javid had been by my side for nearly two weeks. No wonder they behaved as if they'd known me forever.

Dr. Fiona had to go take care of her other patients, children who were sicker than I was, but I had one last question.

"I was in a coma," I said. "For how long?"

"A week."

I had missed a week of my life. And in that time, I'd been shot, I had an operation, had nearly died, and had been flown to the other side of the world. The first time I had ever flown out of Pakistan was on a private jet to save my life.

The world had gone on all around me, and I knew nothing about it. I wondered what else I had missed out on.

28

We Are All Here Now

When the tube in my throat was removed, I had had another call with my father—one where I could actually speak. He had said he would be by my side in two days. But two days turned into two more.

Dr. Javid arranged a third call to Pakistan. My father promised that the whole family would be there soon—just one more day.

"Please bring my schoolbag," I begged. "Exams are coming up."

I thought I'd be home in no time and would get back to competing for first in class.

The next day, my tenth day in the hospital, I was moved from the ICU to another room. This one had a window.

I had expected Birmingham to look like cities I'd seen on television. Like New York City, with tall buildings and cars and traffic, and men dressed in business suits on the street, and women walking on the streets as well. But when I looked out, all I saw was a sky the color of an old teakettle, rainy and gray. Down below were houses, neat and uniform, calm and organized. I couldn't imagine a country where every house was the same. A country where there seemed to be no sun. Where were the mountains? The waterfalls?

———————

Later that day, Dr. Javid told me my parents were coming. I didn't believe it until he tilted my bed up so I would be sitting to greet them when they arrived. It had been sixteen days since I'd run out of my house in Mingora, shouting good-bye on my way to school. In that time, I had been in four hospitals—first in Mingora, then in Peshawar, then in Rawalpindi, and finally here in Birmingham—and traveled thousands of miles. I had met wonderful doctors and nurses and other hospital workers. I had not cried once. Not when the nurses removed the staples in my head, not when their needles pricked my skin, not when the light was like a dagger in my eyes.

But when the door opened and I heard familiar voices saying *jani* and *pisho*, and when everyone fell upon me, weeping and kissing my hands because they were afraid to touch me, finally, I cried. I cried and cried and cried some more. Oh, how I cried.

And for the first time in my life, I was even happy to see those annoying little brothers of mine.

Finally, after sixteen of the most frightening days of our lives, we were all together again.

———————

After we all stopped crying, we took a minute to have a good look at one another. I was shocked at how old and tired my poor parents looked. They were exhausted from the long flight from Pakistan, but that wasn't all. Suddenly I saw that they had some gray hairs and wrinkles. Had they always had them? Or had this ordeal aged them somehow?

I could tell they were shocked by how I looked, too. They tried to hide it, but I could see the concern in their eyes. They touched me cautiously, as if I might break. And who could blame them? I knew from looking in the mirror that half my face was not working. The swelling had gone down, but my left eye bulged, half my hair was gone, and my mouth drooped to one side.

Meanwhile, I had been so pleased to have my voice back that I hadn't realized that I was still able to speak only in simple, baby sentences, as if I were three years old. It wasn't until I saw the surprised expression on Atal's face that I realized how strange I must have sounded.

I tried to smile to reassure them. *Don't worry*, I wanted to say. *The old Malala is still in here.*

But when I smiled, a shadow darkened my mother's face. I thought I was grinning—but my parents saw something that looked like an awkward, crooked frown.

"*Aba*, who were those people?" I asked.

He understood what I was asking—I wanted to know from him who had done this to me.

"*Jani*, don't ask these questions. Everything is fine. We are all here now." Then he asked me how I was feeling, if the headaches had gone away.

I knew he was trying to change the subject, and although I wanted him to answer my question, I let him.

My father, my proud Pashtun father, was not himself. It was almost as if he had been shot as well; he seemed to be in physical pain.

When we were alone one day, he grasped my hand. "*Jani*," he said, "I would take every scar you have, every minute of suffering, if I could." His eyes filled with tears. "They threatened me many times. You have taken my bullet. It should have been me." And then he said, "People experience both joy and suffering in their lives. Now you have had all the suffering at once, and the rest of your life will be filled with only joy." He could not go on.

But he didn't need to say another word. I knew he was suffering, too. He had never doubted the rightness of our cause—but that cause had taken his daughter to the brink of death.

How unjust the world can be sometimes. Here I was, a girl who had spoken to cameras from around the world—but my poor injured brain couldn't come up with the words for the one person I loved more than anyone else.

"I'm not suffering, *aba*," I longed to tell him. "You need not suffer, either."

I smiled my crooked smile and said simply, "*Aba.*" My father smiled back through teary eyes. I knew that he knew exactly what I was thinking. We didn't need words. We had shared every step of the journey that somehow brought us to this hospital room. And we would share every step going forward.

A little while later my mother joined us. I had just started taking small steps, but I still needed someone to help me in the bathroom. Since that first day, my mother had tried not to stare at my face. But as she guided me into the bathroom, I noticed she stole a look at my reflection in the mirror. Our eyes met for a moment, then she looked away.

Then came a whisper. "Your face," she said. "Will it get better?"

I told her what the doctors had told me: I would have to undergo several surgeries and months of physical therapy, but my face would eventually improve. But it would never be quite the same as before.

When she walked me back to my bed, I looked at my

parents. "It's my face," I said. "And I accept it. Now," I said gently, "you must accept it, too."

There was so much more I wanted to say to them. I had had time to get used to my new face. But it was a shock to them. I wanted them to know I didn't care how I looked. Me, who had spent hours fussing with my hair and fretting about my height! *When you see death*, I wanted to say, *things change*. It didn't matter if I couldn't blink or smile. I was still me, Malala.

"My face. It doesn't matter," I said. "God has given me a new life."

My recovery was a blessing, a gift from God and from all the people who had cared for me and prayed for me. And I was at peace. But while I was in Birmingham watching Shrek and his talking donkey, my poor parents had been thousands of miles away, enduring their own terrible pain.

I had been healing while they had been suffering. But from that day on, our family began to heal together.

29

Filling In the Blanks

The next few days were spent with my parents filling me in on what had happened in the sixteen days between the shooting and our reunion.

What I learned was this:

As soon as the bus driver, Usman Bhai Jan, realized what had happened, he drove me straight to Swat Central Hospital. The other girls were screaming and crying. I was lying on Moniba's lap, bleeding.

My father was at a meeting of the Association of Private Schools and had just gone onstage to give a speech. When he finished and learned what had happened, he rushed off to the hospital. He found me inside, lying on a stretcher, a bandage over my head, my eyes closed, my hair spread out.

"My daughter, you are my brave daughter, my beautiful

daughter," he said to me over and over, as if saying it could awaken me. I think somehow I did know he was there, even though I was not conscious.

The doctors told him that the bullet had not gone near my brain and that the injury wasn't serious. Soon, the army took charge, and by 3:00 PM, I was in an ambulance on the way to a helicopter that would take me to another hospital, in Peshawar. There was no time to wait for my mother, so Madam Maryam, who had arrived at the hospital soon after my father, insisted on coming in case I needed a woman's help.

My mother had initially been told I was shot in the foot. Then she was told I was shot in the brain. Neighbors had flocked to our house in tears when they heard the news. "Don't cry," my mother had said. "Pray." As the helicopter flew over our street, she rushed up to the roof. And as she watched it fly by, knowing I was inside, my mother took her scarf off her head, a rare gesture for a Pashtun woman, and lifted it up to the sky, holding it in both hands as if it were an offering. "God, I entrust her to you," she said.

Poor Atal had found out about the shooting when he turned on the TV after school. And he realized that if he hadn't had a tantrum about riding on the tailboard, he would have been on that bus, too.

Within hours after the shooting, Pakistani TV channels ran footage of me with prayers and poems. As this was happening, I was arriving at the Combined Military Hospital in

Peshawar, where a neurosurgeon named Colonel Junaid examined me and discovered something surprising: The bullet was still inside me. He soon discovered that what the doctors in Swat told my father was incorrect—the bullet had, in fact, gone very close to my brain.

He informed my parents that my brain was swelling and that he would need to remove part of my skull to give it space to expand. "We need to operate now to give her a chance," he said. His superiors were being told I should be sent abroad immediately, but Colonel Junaid stuck with his decision—and it was a decision that saved my life.

My mother prayed throughout the five-hour operation. As soon as she began, she felt a calm come over her. From then on, she knew that I would be all right.

But two days after I was shot, my condition was getting worse. My father was so convinced I would die that he started thinking about my funeral. He tried not to think about the past and whether he had been wrong to encourage me to speak out and campaign.

Two British doctors happened to be in nearby Rawalpindi, and the army brought them in to consult. They were Dr. Fiona and Dr. Javid—and they were the next to save my life.

Dr. Fiona and Dr. Javid said that if I stayed in Peshawar, I would suffer brain damage or I would die. The quality of the care concerned them; they thought I was at risk for infection. Even though she was due to fly back to Birmingham, Dr.

Fiona stayed on and arranged to have me airlifted to another army hospital, this one in Rawalpindi.

Security was tight at this new hospital because of the possibility of another Taliban attack. My family was kept in a military hostel near the hospital and had little access to news from the outside world, since the hostel had no Internet connection. They did not yet realize that my story had traveled all around the world and that people were calling for me to be sent abroad for treatment. It was only when a kindly cook from the hostel brought them some newspapers that my parents found out that the whole world knew about my shooting.

My parents were rarely consulted on what should happen to me when my condition became grave. There was no time. All decisions were made by the army. Dr. Fiona insisted that I be treated overseas for the best care. Eventually it was decided that I would go to Dr. Javid's own hospital in Birmingham, Queen Elizabeth Hospital. But I needed to be moved within forty-eight hours, seventy-two at the most. My mother and brothers had no passports or documentation, though, so the army told my father he would have to travel alone with me.

He was in an impossible situation. If he left the country with me, he would be leaving his wife and sons in Rawalpindi, possibly at risk of attack. So he made a choice: "What has happened to my daughter has happened," he told Dr. Javid. "Now she is in God's hands. I must stay with the rest of my family."

Dr. Javid reassured him that I would be taken care of.

"Isn't it a miracle you all happened to be here when Malala was shot?" my father said.

"It is my belief God sends the solution first and the problem later," replied Dr. Javid.

My father then signed a document making Dr. Fiona my legal guardian for the trip to the UK. He was in tears as he handed over my passport.

Although I don't remember it, my parents said good-bye to me at 11:00 PM on 14 October. It was the last time they saw me in Pakistan, and they wouldn't see me again for eleven days. My father did not want me to wake up in a strange country without my family there. He was worried about how confused I would be, how abandoned I might feel. But he assumed their passports and visas were being processed and they would join me in a matter of days.

He had no idea that a government official delayed their departure to join me because he wanted to fly with them. The wait felt endless.

It was during the earliest days in Peshawar, amid the horror and grief, that my father asked my mother, "Is this my fault?"

"No, *khaista*," she replied. "You didn't send Malala out thieving or killing or committing crimes. It was a noble cause. You should not blame yourself. But the ones who should feel shame are the Taliban, for shooting a child, and the government, for not protecting her."

By that time, the Taliban issued a statement saying they shot me because my campaign was "an obscenity." They said they had used two local Swati men who had collected information about me and my route to school and had deliberately carried out the attack near an army checkpoint to show they could strike anywhere. Their trademark was to kill by shots to the head.

Shazia and Kainat, the other two girls who'd been shot that day, were also recovering. Kainat's arm had been grazed by a bullet, and Shazia had been hit in the palm and left collarbone. Two bullets, three wounds.

I had missed so much! And yet, as my parents told me everything that had transpired while I was in a coma or in my windowless hospital room, it was almost as if they were telling me a story about someone else. It felt as if these things had happened to some other girl, not me.

Perhaps that's because I do not remember a thing about the shooting. Not one single thing.

The doctors and nurses offered complicated explanations for why I didn't recall the attack. They said the brain protects us from memories that are too painful to remember. Or, they said, my brain might have shut down as soon as I was injured. I love science, and I love nothing more than asking question upon question to figure out the way things work. But I don't need science to figure out why I don't remember the attack. I know why: God is kind to me.

People don't understand when I say this. I suppose unless

you have been close to death, you cannot understand. But death and I have been very close. And death, it seems, did not want me.

Apparently, many people had tried to visit me. Journalists, celebrities, and a number of politicians. But the hospital had kept them away so I could heal in private.

One day an important minister from Pakistan came and met with my father.

He said the government had turned the country upside down to find the man who shot me. My father held his tongue, but he knew this was empty talk. They had never even found the person who had killed Benazir Bhutto.

Only one person was in jail after the shooting—our poor dear bus driver. The army said they were holding him so they could identify the gunmen. But why had they arrested our bus driver and not the gunmen? It was madness.

The minister also asked my father if I could "give a smile to the nation." He did not know this was the one thing I could not do. My father was unhappy, but, again, he held his tongue. My father, who had dared to talk back to the Taliban, was learning that sometimes saying nothing speaks just as loudly.

When I finally watched the news, I learned that a spokesman for Fazlullah said the Taliban had been "forced" to shoot me because I would not stop speaking out against them.

They had warned me, they told the press, but I wouldn't stop.

My other crimes? I spoke for education and peace. In their terms, I was speaking for Western education, which was against Islam, in their opinion.

The Taliban would try again to kill me, Fazlullah said. "Let this be a lesson."

It was a lesson, indeed. My mother was right when she quoted from the Holy Quran. "Falsehood has to die," she had told me all those years ago, when I was considering doing the blog for the BBC. "And truth has to come forward."

Truth will always triumph over falsehood. This is the true Islamic belief that has guided us on our journey.

The Taliban shot me to try to silence me. Instead, the whole world was listening to my message now.

30

Messages from Around the World

Fiona Alexander brought me a bag of cards. It was Eid ul-Azha, "Big Eid," the holiday when my family went to Shangla. So I thought, *How nice, friends have sent me cards for Eid.* But how did they know where I was? I wondered.

Then I noticed the postage dates. 16 October, 17 October. These were the days right after the shooting. These cards had nothing to do with Eid. They were from people all over the world wishing me a speedy recovery. Many were from children. I was astonished at how many cards there were.

"You haven't seen anything yet," Fiona said. She said there were eight thousand letters for me. Some were addressed simply "Malala, Birmingham Hospital." One was addressed "Girl Shot in the Head, Birmingham."

There were parcels, too. Boxes of chocolate. And teddy bears of every size. Most precious of all, perhaps, was a parcel sent by Benazir Bhutto's children. Inside were two scarves that had belonged to their mother.

There were messages from government leaders, diplomats, and movie stars. Selena Gomez had tweeted about me, Beyoncé had wished me well on Facebook, and Madonna had dedicated a song to me. There was even a message from Angelina Jolie. It was exciting, overwhelming, and—because my brain was still not working right—confusing.

How did *Angelina Jolie* even know who I was?

While I was in a windowless room, unaware of what was happening in the outside world, the outside world knew exactly what had happened to me. Fiona told me that over two hundred journalists from around the world had come to the hospital to see me. Except for that one day when I tried to watch the BBC, I hadn't seen the news since I had arrived. But now I understood: I *was* the news.

People had been praying for me. Dr. Fiona and Dr. Javid and all the wonderful doctors and nurses in Pakistan and England had saved my body. All these people's prayers and support had saved my life.

How amazing. While I was feeling so alone in this hospital, wondering about my family, worrying about how we would pay for my care, people from all around the world were worrying about *me*! I didn't feel so lonely anymore.

I couldn't wait to get home and tell Moniba about Angelina Jolie!

At the tomb of Mohammad Ali Jinnah, the founder of Pakistan.

With my father at the White Palace in Swat.

School bombing in Swat.

The bus in which I was shot.

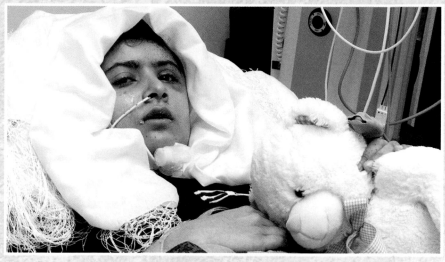
First days in the Birmingham hospital.

I received letters and well wishes from people all over the world.

I am reading in the hospital.

15/10/12   8 pm

Dearest Malala,
Assalamu'alaykum!
You slept this evening after a long journey from Pakistan.
I recited Surah Yasin to you, praying for you and asking
Allah to give you a complete recovery.

I don't feel like leaving you but I have to go home.
I look forward to coming back in the morning to see you
and pray for you again. You are the most courageous
young lady I have ever met! How proud of you your
parents must be – you are an amazing credit to them...

Rehanah ♡

The hospital staff kept a journal for me. This was the first entry.

My friends keep a chair in class for me (far right)
at the Khushal School.

With my father and Atal at the Kaaba in Mecca.

Speaking on my sixteenth birthday, which the
United Nations had declared Malala Day.

At the UN with (from left) Vuk Jeremić, president of the sixty-seventh
session of the General Assembly; Secretary-General Ban Ki-moon; and
Gordon Brown, UN special envoy for global education.

At the Zaatari Refugee Camp in Jordan with Mazoun, a fifteen-year-old Syrian refugee and education advocate.

Sitting with Syrian refugees and praying for a bright and peaceful future.

With my father and Shiza Shahid handing out school supplies to Syrian children at a settlement in Jordan.

The whole family outside our new home in Birmingham.

31

A Bittersweet Day

Doctors operated behind my ear—for nearly eight hours—trying to repair the facial nerve that had been cut by the bullet. This was the nerve that had allowed me to open and close my left eye, raise my left eyebrow, and smile. If they didn't do something soon, they'd said, my face would be paralyzed forever.

It was a complicated operation. First, they cleared my ear canal of scar tissue and bone fragments; it was then that they discovered my eardrum had been shattered. No wonder I couldn't hear! Then the doctors did the delicate work of removing portions of the damaged nerve and reconnecting it.

My job, once the surgery was over, was to do facial exercises in front of a mirror every day. Who knew that such tiny movements could be such hard work? It was four months before I could smile and wink. My parents waited for that moment when I could wink and smile. It was my face, of course, but I thought they would be happiest to have it back!

Every day, I had physiotherapy and had to do exercises, learning to get my arms and legs working properly again. How strange to have to work so hard on something that used to be second nature. The first few times I tried to walk, it was exhausting—like wading through a deep snowdrift.

By now it had been almost a month since the shooting. My family was living in an apartment in a tall tower in Birmingham and visiting me every day. And in a sure sign that life was getting back to normal, my brothers were driving me crazy! I begged my parents, "Leave those two at home! They do nothing but make noise and try to take the gifts I've received."

My brothers had gone from treating me like a china doll (a phase that lasted only a day) to teasing, pestering, and generally annoying me. "What is all this fuss over Malala?" Atal said. "I have seen her. She survived."

I was finally able to read again and devoured *The Wonderful Wizard of Oz*, a book given to me by the former prime minister of the United Kingdom, Gordon Brown. I loved Dorothy's spirit, and I was impressed that even though she was trying to find her way home, she stopped to help those in need, like the Cowardly Lion and the rusty Tin Man. To me, the moral of the story was that there will always be hurdles in life, but if you want to achieve a goal, you must continue.

My language and memory started to come back, too. I was shocked when I looked at the pink notebook Dr. Fiona had given me and saw the questions I had written when I first arrived. Most of them were filled with misspellings and were grammatically incorrect. I still had a hard time remembering some of my friends' names, and I could recall nothing about the shooting. So I worked to show everyone how much I was improving.

My progress was steady and my spirits got better every day.

Finally, in December, after nearly two months inside hospitals, I was permitted my first trip outside. I was homesick for the lush green hillsides of my valley, so Yma, who worked at the hospital, had arranged a trip to the Birmingham Botanical Gardens. My mother and I went with two nurses; my father didn't go, because he had become so recognizable from TV that he was afraid he would attract cameras. On the way, I sat in the backseat of the car, turning my head from side to side to take in everything in a country that was brand-new to me.

I didn't know what the weather would be like outside. I had hoped there would be sunshine, but instead I was met with harsh wind and crisp, cold air. There weren't enough jackets and scarves to keep me warm!

But the plants! They were gorgeous. And strange. And familiar! "This one is in my valley, too," I told one of the nurses. "This one, too!"

I was so overjoyed at being outside it took me a minute to realize that for everyone else at the garden, it was just a normal day out.

My mother was so excited she called my father. "For the first time," she said, "I am happy."

Two days later I had my first visitor from outside the family—Asif Ali Zardari, the president of Pakistan and the widower of Benazir Bhutto. The hospital was afraid of a media circus, but the visit was an essential one. Mr. Zardari had pledged that the government would cover all my medical costs.

So the whole thing was arranged to avoid the journalists. I was bundled up in a purple parka and snuck out of the building through the staff exit. We drove right past a flock of journalists and photographers, and they didn't even notice. It was like something out of a spy novel.

We were driven to some kind of office; and while we waited, Atal, Khushal, and I played a computer game called Elf Bowling. This was my first time playing it, and I still beat both of them! More proof that the old Malala was back.

When the president came in, he was with his daughter, Asifa. They gave me a bouquet of flowers, and then Asifa presented me with a traditional Kashmiri shawl, and Mr. Zardari laid a hand on my head, a gesture of respect in my country. My father cringed a little for fear he would touch the place where my skull had been removed, but it was fine.

Mr. Zardari told us he had arranged for a job for my father in Birmingham. He would be Pakistan's education attaché. He told me that everything would be fine and that my job was to concentrate on my recovery.

Afterward, he said I was "a remarkable girl and a credit to

Pakistan." He was the leader of my country, but he was treating *me* with respect, like I was the VIP!

It was an amazing day. All my worries about how to pay for my care and where my family would stay were lifted.

But, oh, it was a bittersweet day, too. Because I understood: We would not be going home for a long time.

32

Miracles

Finally, I was released from the hospital, and 2013 was off to a happy start. It was so good to be home with my family, even though this home was an apartment in a tall building with an elevator. I would have given anything to be in our humble old house, tapping on the wall for Safina to come play, even taking the rubbish to the dump; but what really mattered was that we were finally together again.

We went for walks in the brisk Birmingham air so I could get my strength back, but I tired quickly. Life in the hospital had been calm compared with all the people and cars and buses rushing here and there. And because I still couldn't hear properly, I was constantly turning this way and that to see what was going on. A simple trip to the grocery store could be overwhelming. Overwhelming—and fascinating.

In the cafés, we saw men and women chatting and mixing

in a way that would be unimaginable in Swat. And in the shops we saw clothing that showed so much skin we couldn't believe the women of Birmingham could wear it without freezing. Here, they wore tiny shorts, bare legs, and high heels even in the middle of winter. "Are their legs made of iron, so they don't feel the cold?" asked my mother.

Sometimes on those early outings, when I saw a man come toward me, I would flinch. If I let my imagination go wild, I could picture every man on the street hiding a gun, waiting to attack. I didn't tell my parents this, though, so they could at least enjoy the chilly Birmingham sights without worrying.

I missed home terribly. I missed my school friends, I missed the mountains, the waterfall, the beautiful Swat River, and the lush green fields. I even missed the messy, chaotic streets of Mingora. So it came as hard news when I found out that there were people in Pakistan who were critical of me. People who said I was a pawn of the West, "hobnobbing" with Richard Holbrooke. People who said I was a bad Muslim. People who even said my father had shot me as a stunt so we could live overseas in luxury.

The other news from home was from school. I was finally able to Skype with Moniba, and for once we didn't fight. She told me how much she missed me and how no other girl could take my place in her heart. She also told me that Shazia and

Kainat were recovered and back in school. And she told me my friends were still saving a seat for me in class.

"Oh, by the way," she said. "You scored a one hundred percent on your Pakistani studies exam." That was the test I'd taken the morning of the shooting. That was the good news. The bad news: Since I hadn't been able to take the rest of the exams, my old rival, Malka-e-Noor, had come in first. Of course she did, since I was not there.

I was falling behind at school! How ironic. The girl who campaigned for girls' education had lost the top spot in her class. Well, I would just have to redouble my efforts so I could take first position when I claimed that empty seat in my old classroom.

Soon, I could walk and talk and read, and my memory was coming back. But I couldn't hear well at all, and there was a constant ringing in my ear. The doctors were also concerned that replacing the piece of skull stored in my tummy might cause an infection.

So more surgery was scheduled—three operations all at once. This time the doctor performed a titanium cranioplasty— which is a fancy way of saying she put a titanium plate in my head. I wondered if I would be like the Tin Man in *The Wonderful Wizard of Oz*: If you knocked on my head, would it ring like a gong? In addition, the doctor who had repaired my facial nerve installed a tiny electronic sound transmitter called a cochlear implant deep behind my ear. Later, he said, he'd fit the outside of my ear with a receiver. The skull piece was also removed from its storage place. These were major operations, but I recovered quickly and was home in five days. (Later, I received a truly special gift—that very skull piece, encased in plastic. I keep it in my bedroom and have been known to show it to guests.)

A few weeks later, when the receiver was situated behind my ear, I heard a tiny beep. Then another one. Then came the sound of the doctor's voice. At first, everyone sounded like a robot, but soon my hearing got better and better.

How great God is! He has given us eyes to see the beauty of the world, hands to touch it, a nose to experience all its fragrance, and a heart to appreciate it all. But we don't realize how miraculous our senses are until we lose one.

The return of my hearing was just one miracle.

A Talib had fired three shots at point-blank range at three girls in a school bus—and none of us were killed.

One person had tried to silence me. And millions spoke out. Those were miracles, too.

33

This New Place

We have settled now into our Birmingham life. We live in a tidy brick house on one of those tidy, tree-lined streets I saw from my window in the hospital. It is lovely. Orderly. Calm. And quiet. Too quiet. There are no children playing cricket in the alleys. No men in the guest room arguing politics. No women on the back porch having a good gossip. My father, who was always "the friend of all friends" to the men in Swat, has many visitors but few real friends here. My mother, who cannot speak English like the rest of us, wanders perplexed through the shops, inspecting the strange foods for sale. Khushal spends a lot of time alone in his room, wishing, I think, for his old life. And the other day I heard Atal, who has the sunniest nature of us all, crying because he had no one to play with. We are just a few feet away from the next house, but for all we know of our neighbors, it might as well be a mile.

As my father says, we live in a neighborhood, but we rarely see the neighbors.

Whenever we go out, people approach us and ask to take a picture with me. I don't mind. I understand that the people who come up to me are the same ones who gave me support when I needed it and who give me courage now to keep going. It's odd to be so well known but to be lonely at the same time.

Meanwhile, we have all adapted, little by little, to this new place. My father wears a handsome tweed blazer and brogues now when he goes to work. My mother uses the dishwasher. Khushal is having a love affair with his Xbox. And Atal has discovered Nutella.

I still go to the hospital for regular physiotherapy sessions to learn how to move my facial muscles. And I'm told I may have more surgery ahead. But I don't think about that too much.

One night our family was out for a walk in the main shopping district in Birmingham. I was marveling at all the different types of people in this city. Unlike in Mingora, where everyone looks the same, here there were all kinds of people: freckle-faced boys in soccer jerseys, black women with long braids, men in business suits and women in business suits, conservative Muslim women in *burqas* and young Muslim women in jeans and headscarves. All of a sudden, a young man called out to my father from behind us.

We turned and I saw that he had the dark features of a Pashtun, but he was wearing Western clothes.

"Sir," I heard him say to my father. "I am from your tribe back home. I know who you are."

My father extended his hand, happy to see a fellow countryman.

The boy pointed at me. "Sir, we all cried for your daughter. We prayed for her," he said. "But what you are doing is not safe."

My father looked puzzled.

"You cannot be out this late in Birmingham," he said. "This city, at night it can be dangerous."

My father and I looked at each other, then we explained to my mother what the boy had said. The poor boy was confused by our reaction. My father hugged him and thanked him. But we couldn't quite explain. How could this quiet, orderly place be unsafe compared with what we had come from?

At my new school here, I wear a British schoolgirl's uniform: a green sweater, striped button-down shirt, and tights and a blue skirt. Most of the other girls wear their skirts short, but my skirt is down to my ankles, and I wear a headscarf as well. Luckily, there are a handful of Muslim girls in my class who do the same, so I don't stick out quite so much. But some of the other girls roll their skirts up even shorter as soon as they arrive at school and let them down again before they go home. And I think: *What an interesting country this is, where some girls are free to cover their bodies and others are free not to.*

Here we also have projectors and laptops, videos and Wi-Fi, and classes such as music, art, and computer science, and even cooking (which I hate). It was a bit of a shock coming from Pakistan, where school was just a teacher and a chalkboard. At times, I wish I were back home, in that simple schoolroom with no computers. But then I think of how my old friends would love all this fancy technology and these special classes. Sometimes I feel sad that my old friends don't have all the wonderful things students have here. And sometimes I feel sad that they have what I don't: one another.

———————

There is something of a gap between me and my new school-mates. Sometimes they make a joke and I don't get it. And sometimes I make a joke and they don't get it. Their man-ner with one another is also quite free compared with the way girls are in Pakistan. I want to join in, I want to have fun, but I don't quite know how. And I cannot be too cheeky. I am expected to be good.

I am a good girl—I always have been. But now, I tell myself, I must *really* be good. So I take extra care with what I say and do. No one else is telling me to limit myself like this. If anything, the teachers here are always encouraging me to be free, to feel at home. But I'm not really free to be like other girls my age—because of the way the world sees me. When you have such a public role and so many people counting on you, I believe you must always act in the way people expect of you.

My life has become extremely busy. I am making books, documentaries, and speeches, and I am meeting interesting people, doing social media campaigns, and engaging in humanitarian work. I get to do so many exciting things and go to so many exciting places, but so much travel while trying to keep up with my studies and exams isn't easy. I am only human and sometimes I get tired. Some days I wish I could just sit on the couch and watch *Mind Your Language* or Skype with friends. But I take the work I'm doing very seriously, always.

I haven't got a best friend here, like Moniba, or even a rival friend, like Malka-e-Noor. But girls at my new school are very kind to me, and I am beginning to make friends. They invite me to go bowling or to the movies or to their birthdays. They are lovely girls. Kind and fun. But it's not the same as it was back home. There I was just Malala. Here, at least at the beginning, I was "Malala, the girl who was shot by the Taliban." I wanted to just be Malala again, a normal girl.

At first, I wondered how I could ever be friends with these girls. I have seen and experienced things they couldn't even imagine. But as time went on, I realized they have had experiences *I* can't imagine. What I'm finding is that we have much more in common than we have different, and every day we learn something new from one another. And every day I feel a little bit more like plain old Malala, just another girl in the class.

But when the day is done and everyone files out for their buses, I think for a moment of the scramble at the end of the day at the Khushal School. I think of how we all tumbled out of the building into the *dyna* that bumped and bounced along the crazy, crowded streets of Mingora.

34

The One Thing We All Know

A few things remain the same in this new world. One: I still fight
with Khushal. (Or rather, he fights with me and I oblige him.)
We fight over who gets the front seat on the way to school. We
fight over what station to listen to on the radio. He tells me I have
a big nose. I tell him he is fat. He tries to give me a punch when
we pull up in front of his school. And I lock the door as he tries to
get out. I may be an advocate for free speech and human rights in
public, but with my brother, I admit, I can be a dictator!

Two: Moniba and I have gone back to our silly old feud-
ing. We Skype as often as we can. But we seem to start each
chat the same way. "Oh, Malala," she says. "You've forgotten
all about me." And I say, "Moniba, you're the one who's forgotten about me."

After we've gotten that out of the way, we get down to having a good gossip.

Sometimes, talking with Moniba and my friends at home makes me more homesick. I can almost smell the wood smoke drifting up from the valley or hear the horns honking on Haji Baba Road. I've seen many other places, but my valley remains to me the most beautiful place in the world. I will go back to Pakistan eventually, but whenever I tell my father I want to go home, he finds excuses. "No, *jani*," he says. "Your medical treatment is not complete." Or "These schools are good. You must stay here until you have learned all you can."

He doesn't say the one thing we all know: It will be a long time before we can go home.

Going home is the one thing we don't talk about, especially now that Fazlullah has risen from the head of the Taliban in Swat to the head of the Taliban in all of Pakistan.

I know this new life is sometimes hard for my brothers. They must feel as if a giant wind suddenly picked them up in Pakistan, blew them across the globe, and set them down here in this foreign place.

As for Atal, he doesn't understand all the media fuss around me. "I don't understand why Malala is famous," he said to my father. "What has this girl done?"

To the world, I may be Malala, the girl who fought for human rights. To my brothers, I'm the same old Malala they've been living with and fighting with all these years. I'm just the big sister.

My mother, though, sometimes treats me as if I'm the baby, not the oldest. She can be very protective, and sometimes, out of nowhere, she will come over and hug me and cry. I know she is thinking about how she almost lost me. Often I catch sight of her wandering in the garden out back, her head covered by her shawl. She feeds the birds from leftovers she keeps on the windowsill, just as she used to do back home. I'm sure she is thinking of all the hungry children who used to eat breakfast at our house before school in the morning and wondering if anyone is feeding them now.

Sometimes my father cries, too. He cries when he recalls those first days after the attack, when I was somewhere between life and death. He cries at the memory of the attack itself. He cries with relief when he wakes up from an afternoon nap to hear his children's voices in the yard and realizes that I am alive.

I don't get angry very often, but I do get angry when people say he is responsible for what happened to me. As if he forced me to speak out. As if I didn't have a mind of my own. If only they could see him now. Everything he worked for over almost twenty years has been left behind: the school he started from nothing, the school that now has three buildings and eleven hundred students. He used to love nothing more than to stand at the gate and greet the children in the morning. The Khushal School carries on—and each day students pass through that gate—but he is not there to see it.

Instead, he goes to conferences on girls' education and he speaks out for peace as he used to do in Swat. I know it's odd for him now that people want to hear from him because of me and not the other way around. "Malala used to be known as my daughter," he says. "But I am proud to say that now I am known as Malala's father."

It's not safe for us to go to Pakistan; that is true. But one day when we were homesick we realized we could bring Pakistan to us. Friends and family come to visit. And Shazia and Kainat, who both go to college in England, stay with us during holidays.

My mother is much happier when she has a house full of guests and extra chairs around the dinner table. As her happiness grows, so does her willingness to try new things. She has begun to learn English again. She has also begun appearing in public without her shawl covering her face and has even allowed herself to be photographed.

My father, meanwhile, has taken on a new responsibility at home. Recently, I teased him that while he and I are busy speaking about women's rights, my mother is still doing the cooking and cleaning. Now he cooks every morning. It's the same thing every time: fried eggs. His cooking is full of love, but not so full of flavor.

He has done some brave things in the past: starting a school without a coin in his pocket, standing up for women's rights and girls' education, and standing up to the Taliban.

But now my brave, proud Pashtun father has taken on the pots and the pans!

35

Anniversary

As the first anniversary of the shooting approached, many journalists came to interview me. They often seemed so sad about what had happened to me. They said things like "You and your family have had to leave your home. You have to live in fear. You have had to suffer so much." And even though I was the one who'd gone through the experience, I wasn't nearly as sad as they were. I guess I see my situation differently. If you tell yourself, "Malala, you can never go home because you are the target of the Taliban," you just keep suffering.

I look at it this way. I can see! I can hear! I can talk! I can go to school and I can fight with my brothers! I am having a second chance at life. And I am living the life God wants for me.

The journalists also ask if I am afraid.

I say no. And that is true. What I don't say is that I am

afraid of one thing: I wonder sometimes if I will be the same Malala in the future. Will I be deserving of all these honors I have been given?

Sometimes when the journalists see my brothers playing so freely, they ask if I am being robbed of a childhood by my campaign for children's rights.

I tell them to think of a girl who is married off at eleven. Or a little boy who has to pick through the rubbish heap to earn money for his family. Or the children who have been killed by bombs and bullets. They are the ones who have been robbed of a childhood.

And sometimes the journalists seem to want to focus on the attack, rather than on my campaign.

This frustrates me, but I understand it. It is human curiosity. Here's how I think of it, though: They have already harmed me, leaving permanent scars.

But out of the violence and tragedy came opportunity. I never forget that, especially when I think of all the good the Malala Fund has done and will continue to do.

We have started a project in Swat for girls suffering from domestic child labor. We support them, so they can go to school and eventually become independent. After months of talking about how much I wanted to help in Jordan, we arranged a trip to help Syrian refugees, many of whom have already missed school for three years. I met children there in dirty clothes with no shoes and only a small bag of possessions. I met children there whom I will never forget. It's our duty to help these children get food, shelter, and an education. And we will.

I think of the world as a family. When one of us is suffering, we must all pitch in and help. Because when people say they support me, they are really saying they support girls' education.

So, yes, the Taliban have shot me. But they can only shoot a body. They cannot shoot my dreams, they cannot kill my beliefs, and they cannot stop my campaign to see every girl and every boy in school.

Millions of people prayed for me, and God spared me. I am still here for a reason, and it is to use my life to help people.

EPILOGUE

One Girl Among Many

On my sixteenth birthday, I was given the most extraordinary gift: I was invited to speak to the United Nations. It was the first of two trips I would make to New York that year. Four hundred people would be in attendance: high-ranking officials from all over the world, such as Ban Ki-moon, the secretary-general of the United Nations, and Gordon Brown, the former UK prime minister, as well as ordinary children like me. It would be a far cry from the solemn and fearful birthdays I had spent in Pakistan not long ago.

My whole family traveled to New York. We saw *Annie* on Broadway, and we stayed in a hotel where they bring pizza to your room on a silver tray. I liked the hustle and bustle of New York, compared with sleepy Birmingham. And I felt as if the city were my old friend after seeing it on *Ugly Betty*. Many people in Pakistan have been told that the United States is a dark and godless place, but everyone I met there was quite nice. I couldn't wait to tell Moniba: America is a very nice place, but it was just as loud and crowded as other cities I've seen, with its honking horns and people rushing here and there. It's like a developed Karachi!

During my second trip, I met one of my favorite people in the United States: a man named Jon Stewart, who invited me to his TV show to talk about my first book and the Malala Fund. He took my campaign very seriously, but he also made funny faces and asked if he could adopt me. I also met the real Ugly Betty, America Ferrara, who is very pretty. And even President Barack Obama and his family. (I was respectful, I believe, but I told him I did not like his drone strikes on Pakistan, that when they kill one bad person, innocent people are killed, too, and terrorism spreads more. I also told him that if America spent less money on weapons and war and more on education, the world would be a better place. If God has given you a voice, I decided, you must use it even if it is to disagree with the president of the United States.)

The day of the UN speech, I was excited.

I'd had amazing experiences and met amazing people. (I'd even meet the Queen of England and Prince Harry and David Beckham one day.) But I was still me. A girl who likes to crack her knuckles as loud as she can and draws pictures to explain things. A girl who hates pasta and likes cupcakes and will always like her mother's rice—and now loves Cheesy Wotsits and fish fingers. A girl who has to stay up late studying for her physics test. A girl who worries if her best friend is mad at her. A girl like any other.

Was it really possible that I was going to address the United Nations? How my world had changed!

I dressed slowly that morning, putting on my favorite pink *shalwar kamiz* and one of Benazir Bhutto's scarves. I had not written my speech with only the delegates in mind. I wrote it for every person around the world who could take courage from my words and stand up for his or her rights. I don't want to be thought of as "the girl who was shot by the Taliban" but as "the girl who fought for education," the girl who stands up for peace, with knowledge as her weapon.

I said in my speech:

Dear brothers and sisters,
Do remember one thing. Malala Day is not my day.
Today is the day of every woman, every boy, and every
girl who has raised their voice for their rights. Thousands
of people have been killed by the terrorists, and millions
have been injured. I am just one of them.
So here I stand...one girl among many.
I speak not for myself, but for all girls and boys.
I raise up my voice not so that I can shout, but so
that those without a voice can be heard.
Those who have fought for their rights:
Their right to live in peace.
Their right to be treated with dignity.

Their right to equality of opportunity.
Their right to be educated.
On the ninth of October 2012, the Taliban shot me
on the left side of my forehead. They shot my friends, too.
They thought that the bullets would silence us. But they
failed. And then, out of that silence came thousands of
voices. The terrorists thought that they would change our
aims and stop our ambitions, but nothing changed in
my life except this: Weakness, fear, and hopelessness died.
Strength, power, and courage was born. I am the same
Malala. My ambitions are the same. My hopes are the
same. My dreams are the same.

One child, one teacher, one book and one pen can
change the world.

As I heard the applause and took my seat, all I could think of was that I had come a long way from Malala the toddler giving lessons to the empty chairs at the Khushal School. And a long way from the girl who gave speeches to the bathroom mirror. Somehow, by the grace of God, I really was speaking to millions of people.

I had once asked God to make me taller. I have realized that God has answered my prayer. God has made me as tall as the sky. So tall I could not measure myself, but my voice could reach people everywhere. I had promised a hundred *raakat nafl* when I'd first asked God to give me height, so I have given him those prayers. But I know that with the immeasurable height, God has also given me a responsibility and a gift: the responsibility to make the world a more peaceful place, which I carry with me every moment of every day; and the gift to be able to do so.

Peace in every home, every street, every village, every country—this is my dream. Education for every boy and every girl in the world. To sit down on a chair and read my books with all my friends at school is my right. To see each and every human being with a smile of true happiness is my wish.

I am Malala. My world has changed, but I have not.

ACKNOWLEDGMENTS

I would first like to thank all the people around the world who have supported me and my cause. I am grateful for every message and prayer I have received.

I am blessed to have been born to parents who respect freedom of thought and expression for everyone. My family is with me every step of the way. My father encouraged me to follow my dream of speaking out for peace and education, and my mother supported us both in this campaign. And my brothers, Khushal and Atal, remind me every day that even though the world knows me now, I am still just their big sister.

I feel honored that I had great teachers and studied in a very good school in Swat. I am and will always be thankful to my teachers for their efforts to spread knowledge and to teach children how to discover talents within themselves and to explore the world. In my new home, I am fortunate to attend the very organized and nice Edgbaston High School for

Girls and to have found such a supportive community. All the teachers (especially headmistress Dr. Weeks) and students have made me feel welcome, and I no longer feel like the confused new girl all the time.

I was treated in very good hospitals in Pakistan and England, and am forever grateful to the doctors and nurses who cared for me. I enjoyed being the patient patient.

I am lucky that I also have an amazing best friend, Moniba. She always guided me to believe in myself and never lose hope.

To be able to share my story is another blessing. Writing a book is a challenging task, and I have many people to thank for helping me through the process:

Karolina Sutton, my literary agent, takes care with every aspect of the publishing process and always has my best interests at heart.

I would not have met Karolina if it wasn't for Shiza Shahid. Shiza also helped to set up the Malala Fund and works every day to deliver our message and grow our campaign for education for everyone.

Patricia McCormick worked with me to tell my story in a new way, and I am grateful for her patience and compassion—and the yoga lesson!

I am thankful to Farrin Jacobs for her hard work in editing. Even though her name isn't written on the book jacket, she did a lot of the work. She made me work hard, but was always working right along with me.

This memoir would certainly not exist without the book

written with Christina Lamb. We have relied on her extensive reporting and research, and I will always be thankful to her for helping me to turn my words into a complete story.

And nothing would have been done if not for the incredible support that Shahida Choudhry provides to me and my family.

Many other people contributed in many different ways, including:

Fiona Kennedy and her team at Orion, my UK publisher; Megan Tingley and Sasha Illingworth and the rest of the team at Little, Brown Books for Young Readers; Megan Smith, Lynn Taliento, Eason Jordan, Meighan Stone, PJ Kadzik, Jahan Zeb Khan, and everyone at the Malala Fund; Norah Perkins, Hinna Yusuf, Ahmad Shah, Mark Tucker, and Tanya Malott; and of course James Lundie and Laura Crooks from Edelman, who have given me and my family tremendous support throughout our new journey.

And thank you, finally, to anyone who reads my story and finds hope and inspiration in its pages. My journey has not always been easy, but I have always believed that truth and goodness will prevail and am thankful above all to be able to speak for those who cannot.

Thank you.

PHOTO CREDITS

Photographs in the color insert are courtesy of the author with the exception of the following:

Pages 6 and 10, top images: Copyright © Sherin Zada

Page 10, bottom: Copyright © Rashid Mahmood / AFP / Getty Images

Pages 11 and 12, top: Copyright © University Hospitals Birmingham NHS Foundation Trust; used with the kind permission of the Queen Elizabeth Hospital in Birmingham

Page 14, both images: Copyright © UN Photo / Rick Bajornas; used with the kind permission of the United Nations Photo Library

Page 15, all images: Copyright © Tanya Malott, provided by the Malala Fund

Page 16: Copyright © Mark Tucker

ADDITIONAL INFORMATION

GLOSSARY

aba: affectionate Pashto term, "father"

Allah: the Arabic word for "God"

al-Qaeda: a militant Islamist organization

Ayat al-Kursi: a verse from the Holy Quran recited to ask for protection

badal: revenge

bhabi: affectionate Urdu term, literally "my brother's wife"

burqa: a garment or robe worn by some Muslim women to cover their bodies in public

chapati: unleavened flat bread made from flour and water

dyna: open-backed van or truck

Eid/Small Eid: a day of celebration to mark the end of fasting during Ramadan

fahashi: indecent behavior

FATA: Federally Administered Tribal Areas; region of Pakistan bordering Afghanistan and governed under a system of indirect rule started in British times

fedayeen: devotees of Islam

haram: prohibited in Islam

Holy Quran: the Muslim holy book

IDP: internally displaced person

imam: local preacher

jani: dear one

jihad: holy war or internal struggle

jirga: tribal assembly or the council of notables of the area

khaista: a Pashto word, meaning "handsome one"

Khyber Pakhtunkhwa: literally "Area of Pashtuns"; until 2010 called North-West Frontier Province, one of the four provinces of Pakistan

madrasa: school for Islamic instruction

maulana, mufti: Islamic scholar

mujahideen: a group of Muslims who believe in jihad or holy war

mullah: an informal name for an imam or a religious leader

mushaira: an event where poets gather to read their poems

nafl: optional prayers

niqab: a scarf or shawl worn by some Muslim women in public, covering part of their face

Pashto: the native language of Pashtuns

Pashtunwali: traditional behavioral code of Pashtuns

pisho: cat, kitten

purdah: (of women) segregation or seclusion, wearing the veil

raakat: particular movements and words that are part of a prayer

Ramadan: a time of inner reflection during the ninth month of the Islamic calendar; observed by fasting every day from sunrise to sunset

shalwar kamiz: traditional outfit of loose tunic (*kamiz*) and trousers (*shalwar*) worn by both men and women

sharia: Islamic religious law

stupa: a mound-like burial structure

Talib: historically, a religious student, but it has come to mean a member of the Taliban militant group

Taliban: an Islamic fundamentalist movement

tapa: a genre of Pashto folk poetry having two lines, the first line with nine syllables, the second with thirteen

TNSM: Tehrik-e-Nifaz-e-Sharia-e-Mohammadi, Movement

for the Enforcement of Islamic Law; founded in 1992 by Sufi Mohammad, later taken over by his son-in-law, Maulana Fazlullah; also known as the Swat Taliban

TTP: Tehrik-i-Taliban-Pakistan, Pakistan Taliban

Urdu: the national language of Pakistan

A TIME LINE OF
IMPORTANT EVENTS

14 August 1947
Pakistan created as world's first homeland for Muslims;
Swat joins Pakistan
The British divide the lands they ruled in colonial India into majority Muslim and Hindu areas to create the states of Pakistan and India. Pakistan consists of two regions, East and West Pakistan, separated by Indian territory. Rulers of princely states, which had remained autonomous during British rule, are given the choice of which country to join. The princely state of Swat joins Pakistan with the understanding that it will remain autonomous.

1947
First Indo-Pakistani War
The princely state of Kashmir, led by a Hindu ruler but with a Muslim-majority population, tries to remain independent

during partition. This leads to internal revolts by pro-Pakistani factions in Kashmir, which are supported by the Pakistani army. Facing the local rebels with Pakistani army support, the ruler joins India in return for armed assistance. The two armies fight for control of the region until the United Nations is asked to mediate. It calls a cease-fire and establishes a line of control based on the positions of the Indian and Pakistani armies in Kashmir.

1948
Death of founder of Pakistan, Mohammad Ali Jinnah
Mohammad Ali Jinnah's death from illness leaves the country without strong leadership at a time when all aspects of the new state need to be organized.

1951
Pakistan's first prime minister, Liaquat Ali Khan, assassinated
Liaquat Ali Khan was another politician who, like Mohammad Ali Jinnah, was key to the establishment of Pakistan. At independence, he became the first prime minister of Pakistan, a position that held more power than that of the governor general at the time (special powers were granted to Mohammad Ali Jinnah). After Mohammad Ali Jinnah's death, Khan tries to stabilize the country by forging alliances and appointing key figures to public office, notably Khawaja Nizamuddin as governor general and Malik Ghulam Mohammad as finance minister. These attempts provoke resentment among opposing political factions, and

Khan instead focuses on winning public support for his poli-
cies. While campaigning at a rally in Rawalpindi, a city in Pun-
jab Province, he is assassinated by an unemployed youth from
North-West Frontier Province. Khan is succeeded by Governor
General Khawaja Nizamuddin as prime minister while Malik
Ghulam Mohammad is appointed the new governor general.

1958
General Ayub Khan seizes power in Pakistan's first military coup

General Ayub Khan, then commander in chief of the armed
forces, takes control of the country in a bloodless coup. President Iskander Mirza is exiled. The coup is widely welcomed by
the population because of the political instability in preceding
years. Ayub Khan sets a precedent whereby the army takes over
the government of Pakistan in times of political uncertainty.

1965
Second Indo-Pakistani War

India and Pakistan clash again over the issue of Kashmir. The
United Nations is again asked to intervene. Another cease-fire
is called, and negotiations are arranged. The United States and
the United Kingdom back the UN resolution by stopping sales
of arms to both countries. Negotiations are held that return
the border to what it was before the war. India and Pakistan re-
nounce the use of force to resolve the issue. These negotiations
are mediated by the Soviet Union and favor neither nation.

1969
Swat becomes part of North-West Frontier Province; Ayub Khan resigns

Ayub Khan loses public support because of his economic policies, which favor the elite; his establishment of a limited democracy with indirect polls, which denied many people their right to vote; and the fallout for Pakistan after the war with India. He resigns, and his protégé, General Yahya Khan, commander in chief of the Pakistani army, takes over. Martial law is declared, and all governing bodies, such as the National Assembly, are dissolved. The government revokes Swat's independent status, and it becomes an administrative district of Khyber Pakhtunkhwa (formerly called the North-West Frontier Province).

1970
Pakistan's first national elections held

These are the first elections held in Pakistan, where every citizen has the right to vote. The Awami League, based in East Pakistan, and Zulfikar Ali Bhutto's Pakistan People's Party, based in West Pakistan, are the major contenders. The Awami League wins the elections. The People's Party has a majority in West Pakistan.

1971
Third Indo-Pakistani War; East Pakistan becomes independent Bangladesh

The Awami League, with its power base in East Pakistan, is entitled to form the government, but Zulfikar Ali Bhutto resists this.

General Yahya Khan supports Bhutto as the formation of the government by the Awami League will transfer political power to East Pakistan. When negotiations between Yahya Khan and the leaders of the Awami League fail, widespread protests erupt in East Pakistan and the Awami League proclaims independence from West Pakistan. In anticipation of civil unrest, units of the army with ties to West Pakistan have been posted in East Pakistan. They are ordered to quell the violence. India supports the formation of the new state and sends its army to aid the Awami League. Fighting spreads to West Pakistan, including the disputed Kashmir border. The government of Pakistan surrenders, and East Pakistan emerges as an independent country, Bangladesh.

1971

Zulfikar Ali Bhutto becomes first elected prime minister

Unable to win the war with India and having lost East Pakistan, General Yahya Khan resigns after appointing a civilian government led by Bhutto, whose party had won the majority of votes in West Pakistan in the 1970 general election.

1977

General Muhammad Zia-ul-Haq takes power in military coup

Bhutto's policies make him unpopular. As a result, he calls for general elections in 1977. He emerges the winner but is accused of massive vote-rigging. Amid civil unrest, General Muhammad Zia-ul-Haq stages a military coup.

1979
Zulfikar Ali Bhutto hanged; Soviet invasion of Afghanistan

Accused of attempting to murder a political opponent, Bhutto is found guilty and hanged. Afghanistan is in the midst of a civil war, as the government wants to move away from Muslim tradition and modernize. In response to this, a Muslim guerrilla fighting force, the *mujahideen*, has risen up against the government. The Soviet Army arrives in Kabul, the capital, to support the government of Afghanistan. The United States, concerned about the spread of communism and the shifting balance of power in the Cold War, looks for allies in the region. As a result, US-Pakistani relations improve, and Pakistan helps the United States support the *mujahideen* indirectly in its efforts to stop the establishment of a communist government in Afghanistan.

1988
General Muhammad Zia-ul-Haq and senior army officers killed in plane crash; elections held; Benazir Bhutto becomes first female prime minister in Islamic world

General Muhammad Zia-ul-Haq's administration generally favors the elite, in particular, high-ranking military officers. His self-appointed prime minister, Muhammad Khan Junejo, however, implements policies, locally and internationally, that conflict with Zia-ul-Haq's agenda. To counter Junejo, Zia-ul-Haq declares a state of emergency and dismisses the government. A little over two months later, Zia-ul-Haq dies in a plane crash along with many high-ranking members of the government and army. Sabotage is suspected; however, no findings are ever made public. The head of the Senate, Ghulam Ishaq Khan, is appointed president until elections can be held. In the elections that follow Zia-ul-Haq's death, the Pakistan People's Party, led by Benazir Bhutto, the daughter of Zulfikar Ali Bhutto, emerges victorious and forms the government.

1989
Soviet withdrawal from Afghanistan complete
Unable to defeat the *mujahideen*, who are being supported by Pakistan and the United States, the Soviet forces withdraw from Afghanistan. The different factions of the *mujahideen* turn on one another, further destabilizing the country.

1990
Benazir Bhutto government dismissed
President Ghulam Ishaq Khan dismisses the government of Benazir Bhutto on the basis of alleged corruption and incompetence. The National Assembly is dissolved, and a state of emergency is declared.

1991
Nawaz Sharif becomes prime minister

1993
Army forces Nawaz Sharif and Ghulam Ishaq Khan to resign; second Benazir Bhutto government

Political rivalry between President Ghulam Ishaq Khan and Prime Minister Nawaz Sharif brings the government to a standstill. The army intervenes and forces both to resign. In the resulting elections, Benazir Bhutto establishes her second government.

1996
Taliban take power in Kabul

After years of civil war among the various factions of the *mujahideen* in Afghanistan, the Taliban, one of the splinter groups, take over Kabul. Although they impose very strict Muslim law on the country, they are seen as a stabilizing influence and are therefore supported by the Bhutto government.

1996
Second Benazir Bhutto government dismissed

President Farooq Leghari dismisses Bhutto's second government because of allegations of corruption and mismanagement.

1997
Nawaz Sharif forms second government; Malala is born in Swat

After being appointed prime minister for the second time, Sharif takes away the president's power to dismiss the government and appoint the army chief of staff. He is, therefore, more secure during his second term in office.

1998

India conducts nuclear tests; Pakistan does the same

India and Pakistan conduct nuclear tests despite the international trend toward nonproliferation of nuclear weapons. This receives international criticism, as the world fears an arms race and nuclear conflict between the two countries. International sanctions are imposed on both countries, most notably by the United States.

1999

Benazir Bhutto and her husband, Asif Ali Zardari, are convicted of corruption; Bhutto goes into exile; Zardari is jailed; General Pervez Musharraf takes power in a coup

Benazir Bhutto and her husband, Asif Ali Zardari, are convicted of the corruption charges that led to the dismissal of her second government in 1996. They are sentenced to five years' imprisonment and a fine, but Bhutto, who is in London at the time of her conviction, remains in exile. Zardari, who is under arrest at the time of his conviction, after being charged in connection with the murder of Bhutto's brother, is imprisoned for corruption. Faced with heavy opposition, Nawaz Sharif fears another coup by the army, the only institution not under his control. He attempts to replace General Pervez Musharraf, the army chief of staff, with a more compliant officer. Musharraf orders the army to take control of government institutions and declares himself chief executive. Musharraf suspends the constitution, dismisses governing bodies, and establishes a National Security Council consisting of military and civilian appointees to run the country.

2001
Al-Qaeda 9/11 attacks on World Trade Center and Pentagon; US bombing of Afghanistan starts; Taliban government overthrown; Osama bin Laden escapes to Pakistan

Pakistan publicly allies with the United States in the war against terror amid international pressure. However, because of the porous nature of the shared border with Afghanistan, many people, including militants, enter Pakistan. Osama bin Laden also covertly enters Pakistan by this route.

2004
Pakistani army starts operation against militants in FATA; first attack on Pakistan by US drone; Zardari goes into exile

The Federally Administered Tribal Areas (FATA) are populated by Pashtun tribes, which maintain their traditional forms of leadership with minimal intervention by the Pakistani government. As these areas share a border and strong cultural ties with Afghanistan, al-Qaeda members are able to hide in this region and use it as a staging ground for attacks.

The Pakistani army launches an attack into FATA to remove the militants. They are not successful and sign a treaty with the militant leader Nek Muhammad Wazir. This sets a precedent for negotiating with the Taliban in the area and undermines the historical tribal system. Nek Muhammad Wazir does not keep the terms of the treaty. A US drone kills him. Released on bail from jail, Zardari goes into exile in the United Arab Emirate of Dubai.

2005
Maulana Fazlullah starts radio stations in Swat; massive earthquake in Pakistan kills more than 70,000 people

The Tehrik-e-Nifaz-e-Sharia-e-Mohammadi (TNSM) movement started by Sufi Mohammad wants *sharia*, or Islamic law, enforced in Swat. After Sufi Mohammad is imprisoned, Maulana Fazlullah, his son-in-law, takes over the TNSM. He starts dozens of illegal radio stations through which he preaches *jihad*, or holy war. He eventually allies with the Tehrik-i-Taliban Pakistan, the Pakistani arm of the Taliban, who want to impose *sharia* across the country.

2007
Army storms Red Mosque in Islamabad; Benazir Bhutto returns to Pakistan; Fazlullah sets up Islamic courts; Musharraf sends troops into Swat; official launch of Pakistan Taliban; Benazir Bhutto assassinated

The clerics of the politically affiliated Red Mosque, or *Lal*

Masjid, a pro-Taliban mosque and madrasa in Islamabad, the capital of Pakistan, encourage violent acts to further their agenda. Female students carry out many acts of civil disobedience. As these attacks escalate, including the taking of hostages, the police and army are forced to take action. A standoff occurs between the *Lal Masjid* clerics (and their followers) and the army. It lasts eight days and results in over fifty casualties. Fazlullah calls on his followers to take up arms against the army for this action. Under pressure to restore democracy, Musharraf allows Benazir Bhutto to return to Pakistan. It is widely believed that an agreement between the two has been reached whereby Bhutto will become prime minister and Musharraf will remain in power for another term as president. Bhutto is assassinated while campaigning for the election in Rawalpindi, Punjab.

2007–2009
Taliban extend influence across Swat

In retaliation for the events at *Lal Masjid*, Fazlullah increases violent attacks in an attempt to impose *sharia* in Swat. After the elections in 2008, a treaty is negotiated between the Taliban and the Pakistani government to restore peace in the area. The Taliban do not adhere to the terms of this treaty, and violence against the Pakistani government, army, and civilians continues. The army launches an offensive, which only escalates the violence. The government agrees to implement *sharia* in parts of Swat. Fazlullah declares a cease-fire.

2008
Zardari becomes president; Musharraf goes into exile
The Pakistan People's Party wins the elections in the wake of Benazir Bhutto's assassination. The party leadership is taken over by her son, Bilawal, and her husband, Zardari, who is elected president.

15 January 2009
All girls' schools in Swat to close by this date, as announced previously by Fazlullah

February 2009
Pakistani government agrees to peace accord with Taliban; the *New York Times* posts a documentary called *Class Dismissed*
After failed military action in the area, which leads to increased violence, the government agrees to another peace treaty with the Taliban. The peace accord imposes *sharia* in the region in return for a cease-fire. This essentially puts the region under Taliban control. A *New York Times* documentary, filmed a month earlier, introduces the terror the Swat Valley faces as it follows Malala and her father and shows their desire to improve education for girls. The documentary helps to gain international attention for the cause.

April 2009
Agreement breaks down as Taliban take over Swat

Fazlullah breaks the terms of the agreement and starts extending his area of control. The Taliban take over the main town of Swat, Mingora, and then the districts of Buner and Shangla, which take them very close to the federal capital, Islamabad.

May 2009
Pakistani army starts military operation against Taliban in Swat; Malala, along with her family and 800,000 others, leaves Swat

The threat to the capital, Islamabad, causes the military to take decisive action in Swat. Two-thirds of the population of the Swat Valley flee the region.

July 2009
Pakistani government declares Taliban cleared from Swat

The military action clears Swat of the Taliban. Maulana Fazlullah escapes the authorities.

December 2009
President Obama announces 33,000 extra troops for Afghanistan, putting the total number of NATO troops at 140,000

2010
Floods across Pakistan kill 2,000 people

The floods are the worst in Pakistan's history. About twenty million people are affected, and a fifth of the country is inundated.

2011
Governor of Punjab Salmaan Taseer assassinated; Osama bin Laden killed in Abbottabad; Malala wins Pakistan National Peace Prize

Salmaan Taseer's assassin, one of his own bodyguards, confesses. He explains that he was angered by Taseer's opposition to Pakistan's blasphemy laws. This shocks the international community because it brings to light the intolerance against non-Muslim communities in Pakistan. Osama bin Laden is killed near Abbottabad in Khyber Pakhtunkhwa Province in a US military operation. The government is widely criticized for allowing US incursion on Pakistani soil and for the breakdown of intelligence that allowed bin Laden to live in Pakistan anonymously.

9 October 2012
Malala shot

Amid increasing threats to her and her family, Malala continues to attend the Khushal School. On her way home from school on 9 October, Malala is targeted and shot along with two other girls on her school bus. Fazlullah of the Taliban claims responsibility. All three girls survive.

2013
Musharraf returns and is arrested; elections go ahead despite Taliban violence; Nawaz Sharif wins to become prime minister for third time

Musharraf is arrested on the charge of overstepping his authority while in power. Allegations include unlawfully detaining members of the judiciary. His arrest shows a marked change in the culture of Pakistan, where previous military leaders were not held accountable for their actions while in power. For the first time in Pakistan's history, a democratically elected government has completed its term and transferred power to another democratically elected government.

12 July 2013
Malala addresses the United Nations in New York on her sixteenth birthday and calls for free education for all children

From her new home in Birmingham, England, Malala attends school and continues her campaign for education for children in every country.

A NOTE ON THE MALALA FUND

Across the world, there are millions of girls and boys who never get to go to school. Just like you and me, they have big dreams and they want to grow up to a bright future. But they never get a chance to have a better life.

I know that you and I can change that. *We* can change that. That is why we started the Malala Fund.

One of my goals in writing this book was to raise my voice on behalf of all those children who cannot speak for themselves. I hope my story inspires girls especially to embrace the power within themselves. But my mission doesn't end there: The Malala Fund believes that every girl, and boy, has the right to get a quality education.

In many countries, it costs just one dollar a day to send a child to school, and fifty dollars can help a girl in poverty get a full scholarship so she can learn. There are so many ways we can help, if we only decide to care enough.

So let's stand together. Let's pledge to each support at least one child who is deprived of going to school. Hold a bake sale on the weekend. Or ask other students to join you and help those who want to go to school but cannot. Or simply speak up for those who are not heard.

Together, we can create a world where every child has the opportunity to go to school and realize their potential.

You can join us and learn more at malalafund.org/voice.

Together, we will be heard.

Malala

ABOUT THE AUTHORS

MALALA YOUSAFZAI started her campaign for girls' education at the age of ten when the Swat Valley was being attacked by terrorists and education was threatened. Using the pen name Gul Makai, she wrote about life under the Taliban for BBC Urdu. Malala also volunteered to be featured in a *New York Times* documentary about education in Pakistan. She used every opportunity to speak publicly for peace and every child's right to an education.

In October 2012, Malala was targeted by the Taliban and was shot while returning home from school. She survived and continues her campaign for education.

In 2011, in recognition of her courage and advocacy, Malala was nominated for the International Children's Peace Prize and won Pakistan's first National Youth Peace Prize. She is the youngest person ever nominated for a Nobel Peace Prize and has received numerous other awards, including the International

Children's Peace Prize (2013), the Sakharov Prize for Freedom of Thought, and the Amnesty International Ambassador of Conscience Award.

Malala now lives in Birmingham, England, and continues to champion universal access to education through the Malala Fund (malalafund.org), a nonprofit organization that invests in community-led programs and supports education advocates around the world.

PATRICIA McCORMICK is a two-time National Book Award finalist and author of several critically acclaimed novels for young adults, including *Cut, Sold,* and *Never Fall Down.* She lives in New York with her husband. For more information, go to patriciamccormick.com.